Can Britain lead in Europe?

Charles Grant

ABOUT THE AUTHOR

Educated at the universities of Cambridge and Grenoble, Charles Grant started to write for *Euromoney*, the financial magazine, in 1981. He joined *The Economist* in 1986, becoming a City reporter and then, from 1989, Brussels correspondent. His biography of Jacques Delors, *Delors: Inside the House that Jacques built*, was published in 1994. In the same year he became defence editor of *The Economist*. In January 1998 he left to become the first director of the Centre for European Reform.

AUTHOR'S ACKNOWLEDGEMENTS

I would like to thank Alex Ashbourne, Lionel Barber, Dan Bilefsky, Colin Budd, Martin Donnelly, Maurice Fraser, Kirsty Hughes, Graham Leicester, Roger Liddle, Lisa Stephenson and Fiona Strain for either reading drafts or being particularly helpful in other ways. My apologies to those I have forgotten to mention. I would like to give a special thanks to Ben Hall, who contributed large parts of several sections.

Contents

1 Introduction

Britain should join France and Germany in forming a triple alliance to lead the European Union, suggested Gerhard Schröder, the German Social Democrats' candidate for Chancellor, in April 1998. Joshka Fischer, the leader of the German Green Party, reacted swiftly. "If he [Schröder] tried to widen the Franco-German relationship into a triangle with Britain it would be a disaster for Europe," said Mr Fischer. "Britain just doesn't know what it wants." He said that Britain's ambivalent position on the single currency and its eager backing of the United States in the recent crisis over Iraq reflected attitudes that had very little to do with the deepest reflexes of France, Germany or their continental partners.

Mr Fischer said in public what several continental leaders say in private. They feel much good will towards Tony Blair's government. But they think it faintly ridiculous for Mr Blair and his ministers to talk of Britain playing leading role in Europe. They believe that Britain's peripheral geographical position, its Atlanticist and Westminster-centred historical traditions, the Eurosceptical bent of much of its public opinion, the absence of any British vision of the kind of Union it wants and, above all, its decision not to join the first group of countries in the euro all prevent it from being a leading member.

All those arguments have force. But the contention of this booklet is that while Britain cannot in the near future be one of the more influential EU members it can in the longer run count as much as any country. Such an outcome will certainly be difficult to achieve. Few Britons appreciate how low Britain's stock with its European partners had sunk prior to the last election.

John Major's government caused even more vexation than Margaret Thatcher's, because of its weakness and lack of direction. His inability to get the Maastricht treaty through the House of Commons in 1992; his threat, in 1994, to block the admission to the EU of Austria, Finland and Sweden, because of his demand for new voting rules that would make it harder to pass legislation, followed by his climbdown; and his vetoing in the same year of Jean-Luc Dehaene, the Belgian prime minister, as Commission president all ensured that Britain remained friendless.

And then in 1996, when BSE made British beef a health hazard, Mr Major decided to block all EU decisions until the ban on British beef exports was lifted. No EU leader had been so disruptive since General de Gaulle left an empty chair in the Council of Ministers for six months in 1965, in an attempt to curb the Commission's growing authority. De Gaulle achieved his objective: the "Luxembourg compromise" allowed any government to block a measure which it considered to be against its fundamental national interests. But Mr Major, not being de Gaulle, had to make another ignominious retreat, removing the veto after three months.

Throughout these years, a steady stream of anti-EU rhetoric flowed from senior ministers. "I hope my fellow heads of government will resist the temptation to recite the mantra of full economic and monetary union as if nothing had happened," wrote John Major in the pages of *The Economist* after the currency crises of 1992 and 1993. "If they do recite it, it will have all the quaintness of a rain dance and about the same potency...the plain fact is that EMU is not realisable in the present circumstances and is therefore not relevant to our economic difficulties."[1]

[1] The Economist, 25.9.93

Between them, Margaret Thatcher and John Major bequeathed a massive legacy of mistrust. Indeed, if there is one thing that holds together the Franco-German alliance—however tattered and twisted that has become of late—it is that the French and the Germans know that when the chips are down they can normally trust each other to do what is right for the cause of Europe, in a way that they cannot trust the British.

None of this means that restoring British influence is an impossible task. Much of the continent is moving slowly towards an Anglo-Saxon model of capitalism, with a greater emphasis on, for example, equity as opposed to debt finance, shareholder value and flexible labour markets. The relative economic success of Britain, compared with the high unemployment that still plagues much of the continent, strengthens Mr Blair's hand. So, undoubtedly, does his government's popularity at home, and the kudos that he has won from the Northern Ireland settlement. With President Chirac looking weak and tired, and Chancellor Kohl apparently on the way out, the EU is suffering from a leadership vacuum.

Europe's future has never looked so uncertain. Many of the forces which in the past ensured stability—such as the Cold War, America's military presence and a solid Franco-German alliance—have either disappeared or weakened. And there is a multiplication of forces promoting change and uncertainty: the advent of the euro; the enlargement of the EU into Eastern Europe; economic crises in Russia, Asia and elsewhere; and political instability in the Balkans, the Eastern Mediterranean and North Africa. But some of these challenges also present opportunities. The EU's structures and future direction are far from set in stone and could be moulded by a country or group of countries that was capable of exerting leadership.

Britain's ability to set the EU's agenda will evidently be limited, so long as it remains outside monetary union. But to minimise that loss of influence, until such time as it embraces the euro, Britain needs to work out a bridging strategy that plays to its strengths. A crucial part of that bridging strategy must be to give a clear indication that, even though Britain will not be in EMU on 1 January 1999, it is preparing to join early in the next parliament.

The bridging strategy will require several other pillars: championing EU enlargement, while recognising that its institutional implications cannot be ignored; stressing the need for economic reform in Europe, while avoiding smugness over Britain's relative economic success; being prepared to take part in more co-operation on justice and home affairs; helping to build more effective mechanisms for co-ordinating foreign policy; and giving the EU a defence identity, without undermining the Atlantic alliance.

The government cannot shape the EU in ways that suit British interests unless it develops a clearer view of the kind of Europe it wants. What should be the institutional architecture when the EU has 25 members? What should be the relationship between the countries in the euro block and those outside? How should Britain respond to Franco-German dominance of the European Union? Should Britain seek to form long-term alliances with other member-states, and if so, with which? Encouragingly, in the summer of 1998, the government started to debate these kinds of question.

This booklet argues that one British objective should be to avoid a "two-speed" Europe. The EU's members should not be divided into sheep and goats, those in the euro and those outside, for an enlarged Union of up to 25 countries will require more fluid and flexible structures. Britain should also search for new ways of making the institutions less distant from and intimidating to ordinary people. The Commission, in particular, needs to be made democratically accountable. However, British politicians will not be able to achieve these or any other objectives unless they learn a skill at which they have seldom excelled: winning friends and making allies among their EU partners.

This booklet does not attempt a comprehensive overview of Britain's relations with the European Union, nor of every EU policy area. The intention is to put forward some ideas for improving Britain's relationship with the EU and for reforming the Union itself, in the hope of stimulating debate.

2 Repairing the damage

"Only four members of the cabinet have any interest in or knowledge of the European Union," said one member of the Labour government—who placed himself among the four—shortly after it took power in May 1997. But the Labour Party is probably no more inward-looking than most other European socialist parties. Long years in opposition give a party few opportunities to develop foreign contacts. If Germany's Social Democrats return to power this autumn—as seems likely at the time of writing—they will be hard-pushed to find four ministers who know anything about the EU.

Having taken office with a commitment to restore Britain's position in Europe, the Labour government has only partially succeeded. Mistakes have been made and the inexperience of the ministerial team has shown. But a large part of the problem has been structural and cannot be blamed on the government's performance. For it came to power just at the moment when 11 other countries were preparing to launch monetary union, a project which will have momentous consequences for the Union and which alarms many Britons. The fact that British public opinion remains broadly hostile to further European integration inevitably limits the policy options available to the government.

As the government gained experience it began to handle European policy with increasing aplomb. But even in the early months Tony Blair and his ministers did much to heal Britain's wounded relationship with its European partners. The prime minister's constructive contributions to the June 1997 Amsterdam summit, such as his signature of the Social Chapter, and the absence of anti-Brussels rhetoric have impressed continental governments. So, too, have Gordon Brown's October 1997 statement on the euro that, "if it works economically, it is, in our view, worth doing"; the decision to introduce proportional representation for the next European elections, to bring Britain into line with the rest of the Union; the fact that British ministers have frequently travelled to the European Parliament to answer questions on Council of Ministers business; and the competence with which Robin Cook and other ministers handled the British presidency of the EU in the first half of 1998.

Some observers claim that Labour's policies on Europe are in practice little different from the Conservatives'. The style rather than the substance has changed, they say. One answer is that style matters in EU politics. Britain's confrontational political traditions may account for the fact that Conservative ministers were often rude to their continental colleagues. Norman Lamont, when chancellor of the exchequer, used to boast about how abrasive he had been in the Council of Ministers. But that kind of behaviour does more to impair than augment British influence. If British ministers speak in a civil manner, show that they can listen and socialise after meetings, those from other governments are more likely to go out of their way to help them. Labour ministers have generally behaved in a more house-trained manner than their predecessors.

A second answer is that the political philosophy underpinning British policies has shifted. Labour ministers are much less obsessed than their predecessors with national sovereignty. At the Amsterdam summit, for example, Tony Blair was prepared to accept the introduction of qualified majority voting, in place of unanimity, into more areas of legislation than were some of the other leaders. Foreign Office officials note that, under the Conservatives, any initiative that might have had implications for sovereignty was soon vetoed. This is not the approach of Labour. As Mr Blair said in his speech to the French National Assembly, in March 1998:

> I have little doubt that Europe will in time move closer still...we integrate where it makes sense to do so; if not we celebrate the diversity which subsidiarity brings. In economic union, in trade and the single market, in the conditions of competition, it makes complete sense for us to co-operate ever more closely. How can we tackle the environmental challenges, pollution and the degradation of our planet, except together? How can we defeat organised crime and the menace of drugs other than together? In all these areas, co-operation and integration over time is sensible and is clearly in our self-interest.

He then went on to say that in areas such as education, health, welfare, personal tax and matters affecting culture and identity, the EU would not get involved. At one level, all this states the obvious. One would have to be an extreme nationalist or an extreme federalist to disagree with the prime minister's analysis. But the preceding government, in its last few years, was not pragmatic enough to consider any policy that could conceivably lead to a notional loss of sovereignty, whatever its potential benefits.

And that is why Labour's approach to EMU, cautious though it is, is fundamentally different from the Conservatives'. The over-riding issue for the prime minister and his chancellor is the economic benefit. They acknowledge that EMU would entail some loss of sovereignty but say that, if the economic benefits are unambiguous, that is a loss worth bearing. The Conservatives' Michael Portillo takes the opposing view that, even if the euro brought economic benefits (and he believes that it would not) Britain should not give up monetary sovereignty.

And yet, despite the government's more constructive European policy, its relations with its EU partners were sometimes fraught during its stint in the EU presidency. Labour's stance on EMU remained hesitant. The crisis over Iraq in February 1998 reinforced some countries' doubts over Britain's European credentials. And the government appeared not to have thought much about the kind of EU that it desired in the longer term.

Continental politicians found Labour's policy on the euro puzzling. They were happy when, in October 1997, Gordon Brown declared the government to be in favour of the principal of EMU and called for the country to prepare to be ready to join in the next parliament. But two months later other governments did not understand why Mr Brown battled so hard to gain membership of the Euro-11 Committee, an informal committee of the finance ministers of the euro countries, when Britain never had much chance of admission (however, there was agreement that excluded countries could join in when matters of common concern were discussed, and that Ecofin, the council of finance ministers, would remain the principal forum for EU decision-making).

And they were concerned that, after Mr Brown's October statement, no minister—nor even the Chancellor himself—made any speech seeking to persuade the public of the benefits of EMU. Mr Blair, speaking in the Hague in January, seemed to take a cooler line on the euro than had Mr Brown. "We believe that a single currency can make sense in a single market," said Mr Blair. "There is no insuperable constitutional barrier to our joining. The test is whether the economic benefits of EMU are demonstrably clear and unambiguous."

But by the time of the Cardiff summit in June, Mr Blair's comments on the euro were sounding warmer. He said that monetary union was the "first step" towards creating the conditions for "a long period of economic expansion." The euro's launch would "help to generate stability and growth" and its success was "crucial to high levels of growth and employment".

Then the *Sun* declared, on its front page, that Mr Blair's wish to abolish the pound made him "THE MOST DANGEROUS MAN IN BRITAIN". Thenceforth Mr Blair's public language was more cautious.

Despite reports that, in private, Mr Blair is warmer about the euro than he is in public, there remains some uncertainty as to where he and his ministers stand on this crucial question. The government seems to contain two schools of thought. The first school regards the euro as an unwelcome distraction from the serious business of winning a second term. This school, reluctant to incur the wrath of anti-EMU tabloids, wants the euro kicked into touch for as long as possible. It hopes that the government can remain neutral on the euro until the next election has been fought and won. The other school believes that, if Britain is to join EMU early in the next parliament, it needs to start trying to shift public opinion from its current hostility, so that a referendum can be won soon after the next election. This school does not believe that it is feasible to fight the next election without a clear policy on the euro.

At a technical level, the Treasury, the Department of Trade and Industry and the Bank of England are doing much to encourage companies and financial institutions to prepare for EMU. But so long as the cautious camp appears to have a greater influence on the government's public pronouncements—as appears to be the case at the time of writing—many businesses, particularly smaller ones, will not make adequate preparations for EMU; public opinion is unlikely to shift drastically in favour of the euro; and other member-states will continue to harbour doubts over the Blair government's commitment to Europe.

One of the government's difficulties, as it now realises, is that EMU will be about much more than a single currency. The euro-11 countries will step up their co-ordination of economic policy. Both the provisions of the Maastricht treaty and the more recent Pact on Stability and Growth will ensure that finance ministers spend considerable time discussing each others' budgetary policies. The fact that the European Central Bank (ECB) will be setting a European monetary policy is likely to spur the euro-11 finance ministers to develop a common fiscal stance of their own. Furthermore, the need to represent the currency union to the outside world will encourage the finance ministers to work more closely together.

The euro will increase price transparency and competitive pressures across the single market. That is already making finance ministers less tolerant of one country gaining an advantage by offering foreign companies or investors markedly lower taxes. In December 1997, EU finance ministers, worried that Ireland's low levels of company taxation would lure many businesses to the island, agreed on non-binding guidelines for rates of corporate taxation.

Luxembourg, having built a banking industry on its refusal to tax private investors' interest payments, is coming under renewed pressure to accept EU norms. Governments such as Germany and Belgium fear that, with the advent of the euro, even greater numbers of their investors will see the benefits of shifting savings into Luxembourg. In May 1998 the Commission revived its plans for an EU-wide withholding tax on interest payments, and in July, when the Austrians launched their presidency, they declared tax harmonisation to be a priority. Any moves in that direction will not come quickly: all decisions on tax require unanimity. But the euro-11 countries accept the need to co-ordinate tax policies more closely.

Thus the EMU that Labour is contemplating joining in 2002 or shortly afterwards is unlikely to be the same EMU that it has decided not to join in 1999. It may well be EMU-plus, a package that includes substantial elements of economic policy co-ordination. That is why a country which stays out of EMU and does not declare an intention to join cannot be one of the Union's more influential members.

Some continental politicians are suspicious of the Labour government's close ties to the Clinton administration. When Saddam Hussein barred UN inspectors from sites in Iraq, in February 1998, Britain said that if Saddam did not let in the inspectors it would join an American-led bombing campaign. France refused to back the Americans and stressed the need for a negotiated solution.

Eventually a majority of EU states offered support for the American position. But the evident divisions among the member-states highlighted the Union's impotence as a serious force in foreign policy. As holder of the EU presidency, Britain had a responsibility to try and forge a common position. But it made little effort to do so. The British knew that their own position was so far apart from the French that a common EU stance was unlikely to be feasible. But the fact that the British did not even go through the motions of trying to work for a common position caused genuine offence in Paris and other capitals.

Nor were continental governments amused when Mr Blair went to Washington: in a visit that was dominated by Monica Lewinsky and Saddam Hussein, the British prime minister displayed faultless loyalty to Mr Clinton but said little about his role as president of the EU. Fortunately for everyone, a combination of American military brinkmanship and French-assisted diplomacy allowed Kofi Annan to persuade Saddam to let in the inspectors. But Mr Blair's stance on Iraq aggravated deep-rooted fears in several EU countries that Britain is ultimately an American poodle rather than a loyal European (his instant and unequivocal support for the controversial cruise missile attack on Sudan in August had the same effect, but to a much lesser extent).

Mr Blair's comment in Washington that he wanted Labour and the Democrats to work together to redefine what it meant to be left-of-centre, and that continental socialists should be brought into the discussions at a later stage, only confirmed French anxieties. Subsequently Mr Blair, Mr

Clinton and their advisers held seminars in both the White House and Chequers on subjects such as the "third way" and welfare state reform.

It is undoubtedly the case that Mr Blair, many of his senior ministers and their top advisers appear to be more at ease in North America than on the continent. And yet Britain's close links to the world's only superpower could prove to be a source of strength as much as a weakness in its European policy.

French Gaullists often make the same mistake as British Thatcherites in assuming that Britain faces an either/or choice between the United States and the continent. When Ray Seitz retired from being American ambassador to Britain in 1994, he wrote, wisely: "America's transatlantic policy is not a series of individual or compartmentalised bilateral policies...it is the policy of one continent to another. If Britain's voice is less influential in Paris or Bonn, it is likely to be less influential in Washington."

Mr Blair appears to understand that a crucial task for Britain is to explain the American standpoint to its continental partners, and vice versa. As he said in his speech to the French National Assembly: "I know that some feel that being close to the United States is an inhibition on closer European co-operation. On the contrary, I believe it is essential that the isolationist voices in the United States are kept at bay and that we encourage our American allies to be our partners in issues of world peace and security." In June 1998 Mr Blair showed his fellow European leaders that close ties to the United States could deliver practical benefits: he persuaded the Clinton administration to retreat over legislation penalising European companies which invest in Cuba, Iran and Libya.

The truth is that, in most matters, particularly economic, Britain is and will remain far closer to the continent than to the United States. But military ties pull the other way, with the result that, when war is in the air, the Channel grows wider than the Atlantic. Mercifully, that is rare.

★

Holding the EU presidency gave British ministers a tremendous opportunity to try and sell the Union's practical benefits to the public. That opportunity was to a large degree missed. Tony Blair talked about the benefits of EU membership in speeches that he delivered in the Hague and in Paris, but few ministers followed his example. The government's media managers made little effort to nudge public opinion in a Euro-friendly direction.

Ministers correctly stressed the importance of a "People's Europe" that delivers the things that matter to ordinary citizens, such as a cleaner environment, jobs and lower crime. But that is not enough for a European policy, especially since creating jobs and tackling crime are primarily the responsibility of national governments. And the recent EU agenda for environmental policy, though important—it has covered the follow-up to the Kyoto agreement on global warming, and new legislation limiting car- exhaust emissions—has been relatively thin.

One reason why ministers seldom made major statements on the future of the EU was that they lacked a coherent view on the kind of Europe they wanted. During the previous government the Foreign Office had taken a leading role in developing EU policy. But during Labour's first year it lost that role and seemed reluctant to think strategically on Europe. And it did not help that some of the ministers most closely involved in European matters seldom talked to each other. Some of Whitehall's most senior officials complained bitterly about the government's refusal to work out a line on Europe.

In April 1998, however, the Good Friday agreement on the future of Northern Ireland allowed the prime minister to focus on other priorities. He launched a review of EU policy and, in May, convened the first in a series of seminars, attended by senior officials, to debate the Union's future. Mr Blair ensured that EU institutions were discussed at the June summit in Cardiff, where it was agreed that a special summit in October would discuss ways of "enhancing democratic legitimacy and making a reality of subsidiarity" (that is, the idea that the EU should act only when it is demonstrably more effective to do so at European rather than national or regional level). Later in the summer Robin Cook held his own brainstorming sessions in the Foreign Office, some of which involved thinkers from outside the government.

Peter Mandelson, then Minister without Portfolio, appeared at a meeting of the Club of Three (a private gathering of senior figures from France,

Germany and Britain) in London at the end of June. Saying that he spoke for the prime minister, Mr Mandelson declared that in seven to ten years time Britain should count as much as France or Germany in the EU. He acknowledged that that would not be possible unless Britain joined EMU. He said that in areas such as foreign policy, and justice and home affairs, the EU needed more rather than less integration; but that its institutions had to be reformed first. The following month Mr Blair's first reshuffle promoted pro-Europeans, such as Joyce Quin, who became Europe minister, and Mr Mandelson, who went to the Department of Trade and Industry. For the first time since winning the election, the Labour government seemed ready to think seriously about what sort of Europe it wanted, and how to get there.

3 The dangers of a two-speed Europe

The difficulty of defining an ever closer union

The Labour government would find it easier to develop an effective European strategy if it knew what kind of EU it desired. Indeed, one reason why France and Germany have so successfully shaped the Union to suit their interests is that they have known their long-term objectives—such as EMU—and held to them tenaciously. British policy has generally involved reacting to the initiatives taken by others.

But while the British government should ponder the future shape and structure of the EU, it should not go further than trying to define some general principles. In July 1998, Paddy Ashdown, the Liberal Democrat leader, argued in a CER lecture that EU governments should set down the objectives of European integration in a constitutional document. Then Douglas Hurd, the former Conservative foreign secretary, wrote that a new treaty was needed to define the respective competences of the EU and the member-states for the next 20 years.[2] Their point is that public opinion may fear that the arrival of EMU will push the Union down the slippery slope towards a federal super-state. The way to reassure people that EMU will not have such dire consequences, they argue, is to delineate now what the Union should and should not do.

[2] Prospect, August/September 1998

The consolidation of the existing rag-bag of treaties into a simpler, clearer text that could be read as an EU constitution would certainly be welcome. In practice, however, such an exercise would reopen a Pandora's box of constitutional demons. Because different governments interpret different articles in different ways, the consolidation could not occur without many of the battles of earlier inter-governmental conferences being refought. So it might be more useful for the governments to publish a short, readable summary of the EU treaties, in a format similar to this booklet. That would offer European citizens a better prospect of understanding the EU's important principles and rules, while for legal purposes the existing treaties would remain in force.

However, the member-states should not follow Mr Ashdown and Lord Hurd in trying to define the final destination of what the treaties refer to as "an ever closer union". The first reason is that the Union has not evolved merely in response to pre-programmed instructions left by Jean Monnet, Paul-Henri Spaak and the other founding fathers. External circumstances have accounted for much of the EU's historical development. For example, in the 1980s fear of economic "Euroscelerosis", compared with America's more dynamic economy, was one factor which spurred the Commission to come up with the programme to create a single market by 1992. And it was the reunification of Germany in 1990, and the consequential fears of German strength both inside and outside Germany, that drove forward the plan for EMU enshrined in the Maastricht treaty. External events which are, as yet, unpredictable, will surely continue to shape the Union's progress. For example, if America pulled its troops out of Europe, or if Russia became militarily resurgent, the Union's defence capability would certainly have to be rethought.

The second reason is that the member-states will not, at least for several years yet, be able to agree on what the Union is for. Each has its own rationales and objectives for European integration, and the outcome is inevitably a compromise between the various national priorities. For example when the French pontificate on the future of the Union they tend to talk of Europe as *une puissance* (a power). Long attached to their own state as a defining attribute of Frenchness, they have transferred some of their feelings for it to the Union. Thus the French often say that a good reason for having EMU is that it will make the Union more of a *puissance* and better able to stand up to the United States.

One seldom hears a Briton justifying EMU thus. The British have usually seen European integration in terms of material benefits. Many Britons would accept that the EU is and should be more than a free-trade area; but its essential justification, for most of them, is economic. To many Germans, the EU's great achievement is to weaken and constrain the nationalism that has stained their history, and thus to reassure their neighbours about German intentions. Many Italians admire the EU as a source of honest and relatively efficient administration that contrasts with their own notoriously unstable political system. Thus they are happy for it to impose some discipline, for example on their budgets. And so on.

It is true that there has been some convergence of views on what the EU is for: several of the continental countries, such as Germany and Italy, play down federalism and talk more of the EU delivering practical benefits, while Britain is more willing to discuss further integration. But any attempt to define the final goal could force countries that may be moving away from federalism to veer back to it, at least at the level of rhetoric. Europe cannot harmonise away the peculiarities of its national histories and should therefore not be too precise about defining exactly where the process of integration will end.

Nevertheless the British government should try to map out an overall approach to European integration. British politicians have generally avoided talking about the future of the EU—perhaps because, when they have done so, tabloid newspapers have jumped at them. When Peter Mandelson talked about the circumstances in which sovereignty could be pooled, in a speech in Florence in January 1998, the *Sun* howled the next day that he planned to throw it away.

Mr Mandelson had said:

> *In my experience, there are very few people who worry about the pooling of sovereignty if they think it makes sense and is going to bring them benefits. I have never had anyone turning up at my constituency surgery in Hartlepool to complain about the loss of sovereignty involved in Britain's membership of NATO...People do not worry about it, because they know that collective defence makes far better sense than unilateral defence. They know that pooling of sovereignty gives us in this case some real control over our destiny—whereas, if we were left on our own, we might in practice have none at all.*
>
> *Loss of sovereignty only concerns people if they think they are giving it up to no good purpose. The problem with Europe is that too many of our citizens have only perceived*

the aggrandising ambitions of European institutions. We have not demonstrated clearly enough that the purpose of pooling sovereignty is to address issues that are of real concern to ordinary people's lives.

Mr Mandelson, like Mr Blair in his Paris speech of April 1998, has begun to define the principles of a coherent attitude to European integration. But it is significant that both speeches, delivered outside Britain, were aimed at a foreign audience.

They need to make such speeches to domestic audiences and to become a little bolder. They could reassure those who fear a super-state by pointing out that the nation-state is in robust health and will remain Europe's principal political unit; even Helmut Kohl now acknowledges as much. The EU will continue to be a hybrid beast, a Union of States based on inter-governmental co-operation in some areas and pooled sovereignty in others.

The government should stress that any future moves towards integration will not come about because blueprints set down in the treaties have to be implemented, nor because a closer union is inherently desirable in itself. Its attitude to action at EU level will instead be pragmatic. The involvement of Brussels is neither necessarily good nor necessarily bad. Proposals for integration can be justified only if they are shown in each case to be likely to contribute to the economic well-being, quality of life or security of the people. Furthermore, such integration must be founded on their understanding and consent. That means that every decision at European level must involve an effort of justification and communication.

The inevitability of variable geometry

The two strongest forces shaping the future of the Union are enlargement and EMU. The former, which could lead eventually to an EU of some 25 countries, is essentially a disintegrating force. The latter, which is certain to include less than the full membership of the Union, is a force for integration.

The traditional model of the EU involves all countries subscribing to all the same policies, except for new entrants which may be granted time-specific derogations in some areas. New members are required to join all the Union's "pillars". The first pillar, the European Community (subject to the Treaty of Rome, as subsequently amended), covers the single market, related areas such as free movement and EMU. The second covers the Common Foreign and Security Policy (CFSP). The third covers co-operation on justice and home affairs. Union institutions, such as the Commission, Parliament and Court of Justice play a lesser role in the second and third pillars.

The traditional model cannot survive the Union's enlargement into Eastern Europe. In fact it is already passé. The British opt-outs from EMU and the social chapter at Maastricht; the subsequent Danish opt-outs from defence co-operation and EMU; the British and Irish opt-outs from the "area of freedom, security and justice" (that is, co-operation on immigration, asylum and frontier controls) in the Treaty of Amsterdam; and the fact that Austria, Finland and Sweden, which entered the Union in 1995, do not wish to join the Western European Union (WEU), the EU's defence wing, have, between them, damaged beyond repair the idea that everybody has to do all the same things.

Purists still hope that this "variable geometry" is temporary. The Amsterdam treaty specifies that new members must sign up to all of the Union's objectives and take part in all its pillars. But future enlargements, bringing in a more varied collection of social, economic and administrative cultures, are likely to kill off the hopes of the purists.

Some sort of "variable geometry" is inevitable, to accommodate both countries which wish to deepen their commitment to European integration, and those that do not. Two models of institutional architecture appear feasible. One is that of a two-speed Europe. An advance guard would push ahead with EMU and much else, leaving the slower member-states behind. That was the essence of a controversial paper from Wolfgang Schäuble and Karl Lamers, two senior German christian democrats, in 1994. They advocated a "hard core" of France, Germany and the Benelux countries, and assumed that the lead group on EMU would also push ahead in CFSP and justice and home affairs. A similar concept lay behind Valéry Giscard d'Estaing's idea of differentiating between an inner circle committed to *Europe puissance* and an outer circle content with *Europe espace* (meaning a European economic area). The driving force behind all these ideas is the desire to stop awkward customers—and Britain, in particular—from braking further integration in an area where other countries wanted it by, for example, refusing to accept the extension of qualified majority voting.

A second model is a Europe of multiple cores. This model assumes that EMU is not the be-all and end-all of European integration. Countries which stay out of the euro may nevertheless choose to take a lead in, say, defence or justice and home affairs. This design would not be of concentric circles but of interlocking, Olympic rings.

Both models assume that a wide range of EU policies, such as the single market and related areas, trade, the CAP, the structural funds, the environment and probably foreign policy, would have to be compulsory for everyone. Otherwise such policies could not operate effectively.

The second model would be better for Britain—and also for the East European countries which hope to join the Union. In a wider EU, not every country will wish, or be able, to move at the same speed in every area of policy. A Europe of 25 or more countries will contain such a diverse array of cultures, histories and traditions that it will need fluid and flexible structures. Not a single, monolithic construction, but a Europe of many spires—and even of minarets.

This Europe of multiple cores would allow the wishes of some member-states to opt out of certain areas to be reconciled with the more ambitious goals of others. If the Union insisted that applicants had to participate in all policy areas right from the start, the process of enlargement could well slow down (though the example of Sweden, which qualified for EMU, had no opt out, did not want to take part and was allowed not to, suggests that the euro is one policy area into which new members will not be forced). For example, some applicants might be willing and able to join most parts of the EU long before they were ready for a passport union. In fact several of the East European states may have to opt out of the removal of internal frontiers—either because they wish to, or to satisfy existing members—in order to be able to join the EU by the middle of the first decade of the next century.

Those countries which cannot make the grade on EMU will not want to be branded "second division" and excluded from discussions of other areas of policy. Consider Europe's emerging defence identity, in which Britain—

even if it continues to shun EMU—is likely to be a leading player. Germany will undoubtedly be an influential member of the monetary union, but for all sorts of historical and constitutional reasons it is not going to be in the forefront of European defence policy.

It is crucial that the new institutional structures, built around EMU and other cores, are flexible. Any EU member which starts off outside a core grouping should be allowed to join later, so long as it can meet reasonable criteria. Thus if Sweden abandoned neutrality and wished to join the WEU (or a new fourth pillar for defence), it should be taken in. The countries in the first wave of EMU, too, should not bolt the door after 1 January, 1999, for many East European states will in the long run wish to join.

The danger of a two-speed Union is that the euro core could become detached from the remainder of the membership. It could start to drive policy priorities in areas of concern to all member-states. The governments of the advance guard might well be tempted to strike deals among themselves, possibly to the detriment of the single market's integrity. The delicate balance between EU institutions and member-states could be affected: a caucus of governments, perhaps led by France and Germany, could increase their influence at the expense of the Commission.[3] Managing variable geometry— whether of the two-speed or multiple core variety—may require a Commission that is in some respects stronger, to ensure fair play between ins and outs. For example, the Commission would have to decide whether a group of countries had the right to go ahead in a policy area—and then, later on, whether other countries had the right to join the advanced group. As Brigid Laffan of University College, Dublin, has put it, "Paradoxically, if flexibility is not to fragment the Union, it requires stronger not weaker central institutions." [4]

3 This is discussed in Francoise de la Serre and Helen Wallace, "Flexibility and enhanced co-operation in the European Union: Placebo rather than Panacea?", Notre Europe, Paris, 1997

4 Quoted in "Amsterdam: What the Treaty means", Institute for European Affairs, Dublin, 1997

So is two-speeds or multiple cores more likely to come about? There is some evidence in favour of both models. The Amsterdam treaty does contain provisions for flexibility, in the form of a general clause and articles that refer specifically to the "first pillar" (the European Community) and the "third pillar" (justice and home affairs). In theory these provide for groups of countries to go ahead in certain areas, on the Olympic rings model. In practice, however, the use of the

flexibility clauses is so circumscribed that it is doubtful whether they will
ever be used.

Chatham House's "Britain and Europe" summarises the treaty's
provisions on flexibility admirably:[5]

[5] *Royal
Institute for
International
Affairs, 1997*

> *Under its current construction, it is questionable how far the
> general flexibility clause will permit advanced integration
> among a subset of member-states. Use of the clause is
> confined to very tight conditions. It must involve a majority
> of member-states, and it must not affect the rights and
> obligations of those member-states which do not participate.
> In addition, the reservations placed on its use within the
> Community pillar…leave little room for manoeuvre.
> Flexibility must not affect Community policies or
> programmes; it must not impede trade and competition; it
> cannot affect the exclusive competences of the Community;
> it should not result in discrimination among member-state
> nationals. Furthermore, while flexibility decisions can be
> made by qualified majority voting, any member-state
> reserves the right of veto "for important and stated reasons
> of national policy".*

The areas in which these flexibility arrangements could conceivably be
used are justice and home affairs co-operation in the third pillar, and those
parts of the first pillar that remain subject to unanimity, such as
immigration and asylum, transport, industrial policy and taxation. Several
continental governments have talked of using flexibility to bypass British
opposition to the introduction of majority voting on tax. The treaty
would allow them to establish such a core grouping, if a qualified majority
of all members was in favour, if a Commission opinion said that it was
compatible with the treaties and if Britain (or some other member) did
not wield a veto. The second and third conditions might prove very hard
to satisfy.

If the Amsterdam treaty pointed tentatively to a multi-core future, the
emergence of the Euro-11 Committee may suggest a two-speed Union.
The countries in EMU clearly intend to co-ordinate a fairly wide range
of economic policies. The French are keen to turn the Euro-11 Committee

into a powerful policy-making body, so that a political institution shadows the work of the ECB. They believe that, after future enlargements, it would be impractical for an Ecofin of 20 or more countries to co-ordinate economic policy in an effective and meaningful way. But the Germans oppose giving the Euro-11 Committee such an important role and the French may not get the kind of committee they want.

Those opposed to interlocking rings argue that they would create overly-complex institutional structures; ordinary people could understand two speeds more easily. The multiple cores model certainly has little support among senior figures in the British government. Mr Mandelson worries that the more the EU allows variable geometry, the greater is the risk of Britain being sidelined. So long as Britain remains a semi-detached member, prone to use opt outs, his concerns are understandable. But if the government succeeded in making Britain a more influential member, at the heart of decision-making, it would not have to worry about variable geometry being used against British interests.

There is not much doubt that, on current trends, EMU is likely to become the key issue that defines a country's status within the Union. But the actual shape of the EU in 2010 is bound to involve elements of both models. There will be several cores and EMU will be by far the most important. Whether or not Britain joins EMU, it would be better off in a more flexible Union, and the Union as a whole would be better off with many spires. The more rigid the design of the future Union, the more brittle it will be. More fluid structures are likely to be able to cope better with as yet unforeseen challenges.

4 A bridging strategy for Britain

How can Britain avoid the slow lane of a two-speed Europe? It needs to develop a bridging strategy that maximises its influence during the transitional period between now and when it joins EMU. This strategy must play to British strengths and involve a more enthusiastic attitude to integration, or to co-operation, over a wide span of issues—EMU, economic reform, enlargement, justice and home affairs, foreign policy and defence.

A more positive stance on EMU

The policy of not joining the euro during the lifetime of this parliament appears to be fixed. Without abandoning this policy, however, Mr Blair could take a bolder stance on the euro. He could say that in principle the government favoured joining EMU soon after the next election, so long as certain economic conditions were satisfied. Such a declaration need not necessarily go much beyond Gordon Brown's statement to the House of Commons in October 1997. If Mr Blair was able to dispel the current confusion over Britain's intentions towards the euro it would greatly boost his credibility with other European governments.

As they prepare for EMU, British ministers will have to grapple with the question of what exchange rate policy, if any, they need. Politically, this is a delicate subject. Memories of Black Wednesday, the day in September 1992 when sterling fell out of the Exchange Rate Mechanism (ERM), probably did more than anything else to damage the reputation of John Major's government.

It is not entirely certain that Britain would be able to join the euro without first spending some time in the ERM. Since the ERM was reformed in 1993, to allow each member currency a fluctuation band of 15 per cent (instead of the earlier 2.25 per cent and 6 per cent bands) either side of its central rate, it has operated smoothly. The Maastricht treaty says that, in order to join EMU, a member-state's currency must observe "the normal fluctuation margins provided for by the ERM of the

European Monetary System for at least two years, without devaluing against the currency of any other member-state". The Treasury view is that the drastic ERM reforms of 1993 make that condition redundant. But a majority of governments, as well as Hans Tietmeyer, the Bundesbank president, and Wim Duisenberg, the ECB president, takes the treaty language to mean that sterling must spend about two years in the ERM. They believe that to let in a currency that lacks a track record of stability could weaken EMU.

Leaving aside the Maastricht treaty, there may be practical reasons for Mr Brown to consider rejoining the ERM. Squeezed between the dollar and euro blocks, sterling risks becoming a more unstable currency; indeed, its trajectory in 1998 suggests that that may already be happening. Speculators now have fewer other currencies into which, and out of which they can shift funds. Mr Brown often says that Britain needs a period of financial stability before it can join the euro; the shelter of the ERM might provide it.

In any case, rejoining the ERM sooner would make it easier for Britain to join EMU later. Sterling would have to enter the ERM at a much lower rate than the DM2.90 rate of September 1998. Such a move would also bring long-term interest rates closer to the lower levels of the continent: the markets would assume that the discipline of the ERM, as a prelude to EMU membership, would help Britain to kick the habit of inflation (For most of 1998 Britain's inflation rate has been more than twice the average rate of the euro-11 countries). The policy of rejoining the ERM, if marketed well, need not necessarily be unpopular: manufacturing companies would welcome the competitive advantage of a lower and more stable exchange rate, while the cost of mortgages could halve.

Despite these potential advantages, the government is unlikely to risk popular disapproval by rejoining the ERM. It believes that Britain's partners will ultimately waive ERM membership as a condition for joining EMU. After all, the thinking goes, Italy and Finland are joining EMU after rather less than two years in the ERM, so a country of Britain's importance should be treated as a special case.

"Exchange rates are outcomes not targets: if we do things right and have similar policies of financial stability to our partners—ie low inflation and cheap money—we should get the right outcomes," said a government minister at a CER seminar in February 1998. Several members of the government stress that so long as Britain shadows its partners' policies, the pound should—barring some unexpected shock—be stable against their currencies.

But other government figures are not as confident that currency stability will be easy to attain. In any case, sterling could not move straight from a period of free floating to membership of EMU. As Eddie George, the Governor of the Bank of England, told the House of Commons Treasury select committee in April 1998, if the government decided to prepare for entry to EMU, it would have to instruct the Bank to pursue a stable exchange rate against the euro rather than—as at present—an inflation target of 2.5 per cent. "We would have to draw attention to the potential conflict between the two objectives, and have to insist the objectives be made clear."

It would not be feasible, politically, for the government to switch from an inflation to an exchange rate target until it had succeeded in meeting the former. But as an interim step it could declare in public that if, as is likely, the ECB announces inflation targets, Britain will shadow them.

So long as the government does pursue—and attain—a stable exchange rate for about two years before it wishes to join EMU, it can probably get away with staying outside the ERM. But if the government is serious about joining in 2002, it will need to hasten its legal and practical preparations. Legally, in order to comply with the Maastricht treaty, the Bank of England will have to be made fully independent.

Practically, the government needs to confront some of the peculiarities of the British housing market. The prevalence of floating-rate mortgages makes the economy and public opinion especially sensitive to interest-rate changes. An increase in fixed-rate lending to both house buyers and companies would reduce an important structural difference between the British economy and most of those in the EMU club. Once it became clear that the government did intend to join the euro, interest rates would—other things being equal—fall and fixed-rate mortgages should become more popular. But British borrowing habits do not change easily, and in the past lower interest rates have not led to much growth in fixed-rate borrowing.

The government should talk to the mortgage lenders about the kinds of tax incentive that would encourage borrowers to convert their mortgages to a fixed rate of interest. Such incentives would probably have to be limited to a specific number of years in order to win Treasury approval.

If the government wants to win a referendum on the euro in the autumn of 2001, it must start trying to shift public opinion from its current hostility sooner rather than later. Ministers will have to summon up the courage to stick their heads above the parapet, face the fire of the *Sun* and other tabloids, and spell out both the advantages of joining EMU and the costs of staying out. By September 1998, however, ministers did not appear in any hurry to do so.

During the British presidency this author asked one senior minister why the government had not begun to make the case for EMU. He said that it was crucial to keep the tabloids on side during the six-month presidency. But when is the good moment to take them on? The risk of delaying the campaign to soften up public opinion is that, when ministers do finally get down to it, their government may have less credibility and authority than it does today.

Championing economic reform

People expect the European Union to create jobs. EU institutions cannot do much, directly, to get the Union's 18 million unemployed back to work. Nevertheless if unemployment remains at such high levels in many countries, public confidence in the Union, and especially in its central project of EMU, will be undermined. Britain should promote economic reform, especially on the supply side, so that EU economies are better able to create jobs and make a success of monetary union.

Tony Blair wants economic reform to be a cornerstone of Britain's European policy—and has linked it to his theme of the "third way". He said in his Hague speech of January 1998:

> *Europe has to find its own way—a new third way—of combining economic dynamism with social justice. This third way is more than the free market plus decent public services— laissez-faire economics with a warm heart. It is about active government working with the grain of the market to ensure*

a highly adaptable workforce, good education, high levels of technology, decent infrastructure and the right conditions for high investment and sustainable non-inflationary growth. It is about securing the flexibility that the market offers with the "pluses" that only an active government can add.

The British government is right to argue that much of the continent has something to learn from Britain: unemployment is six per cent in Britain, yet 10-12 per cent in Germany, Italy and France and 20 per cent in Spain. The revival of economic growth on the continent has started to narrow that gap, but much of its unemployment remains structural. And yet, though Britain's relative success at job creation is undoubtedly a source of strength within the EU, the government will have to handle the theme of economic reform with extreme sensitivity. For many continentals are inclined to believe that, despite talk of a "third way" between uncaring American capitalism and old-fashioned state-dominated corporatism, New Labour really wants to impose the harshest brand of American labour market deregulation. Tony Blair did not get off to the best of starts when, at a May 1997 congress of European socialists in Malmo, shortly after his electoral triumph, his exuberant praise of the British model upset leading continental socialists.

In 1998, however, the government has wisely avoided a triumphal tone. In speeches and articles during the British presidency, Mr Blair stressed that Britain can learn from continental successes, such as labour market reforms in the Netherlands and Denmark, where the level of unemployment is comparable to that in the UK. British ministers will certainly be listened to more attentively if they can acknowledge that, in some areas crucial to economic success, such as training, secondary education and infrastructure, Britain has much to learn.

They should probably avoid using the phrase "third way" on the continent. It tends to mean different things in different countries. In much of Eastern Europe in the early 1990s, for example, leftists used the phrase to describe a happy median between Soviet Communism and Western capitalism. When Britons talk of the third way, it may appear as something that is half-European and half-American, and thus unappealing. British ministers would be wise to sell economic reform as a means of modernising and reviving the European social model. They could stress the wealth of good practice that already exists in some parts of Europe and that can be drawn upon to shape the necessary reforms.

The Union itself cannot do much to reform labour markets or create jobs, since they are primarily the responsibility of national governments, but it is becoming a forum in which governments can swap examples of best practice. The special Jobs Summit, in Luxembourg in November 1997, agreed on guidelines for employability, entrepreneurship, adaptability and equal opportunities. Based on these guidelines, governments prepared national action plans on how they intended to combat unemployment and reform labour markets. They reviewed each others' plans at the Cardiff summit in June 1998 and will do so again in Vienna in December. It is too early to judge the impact of this co-ordinated action on employment, but the Commission has played a useful role in providing information, monitoring progress and highlighting shortcomings.

Economic reform in France and Germany must certainly mean liberalising labour markets, notably by curbing the non-wage costs of employment. But as Gordon Brown never tires of saying, improving labour markets also means governments playing an active role in promoting "employability", that is encouraging people to develop the skills, knowledge and adaptability they need in order to find employment.

The chancellor has rightly stressed that economic reform is also about liberalising product and capital markets.[6] The former requires a vigorous and rigorous competition policy at EU level. As he said in Frankfurt in March 1998, the EU needs "a competition policy that creates more dynamic markets, is effective against those cartels and monopolies that hold new businesses and job creation back, and—in areas where European-wide job creation is still inadequate—pushes forward the frontiers of the single market".

[6] *See Gordon Brown, "Britain, globalisation and the new European economy", CER (forthcoming)*

Even with a tough and independent-minded competition commissioner, such as the current incumbent, Karel Van Miert, the Commission's handling of competition cases is sometimes influenced by political considerations. Particularly in cases of illegal state aid, the Commission's attempts to impose fines on national governments often end in unedifying political compromises. Thus in July 1998, when the

European Court ruled that French government subsidies to Air France had been illegal, the Commission refrained from demanding that the money be paid back.

Britain should seek to reform EU competition procedures so that they become less vulnerable to political interference. Directorate-General 4, the Commission's competition department, should publish each case report that it submits to the commissioners for their decision. Then if the commissioners wished to over-rule the official advice, for political or other reasons, they would have to issue a written explanation to the public.

The competitive pressures of the European single market have forced European businesses to modernise and improve their productivity. That is one reason why so many European companies are world leaders. But the market's job-creating potential is still marred by many barriers, both formal and informal. The British government should encourage the Commission to come up with proposals for making the market more effective in areas such as gas, electricity, public procurement and financial services.

Britain should also work to make EU policies more consumer friendly. Consumer groups currently have much less influence on the decision-making process than producer organisations. Thus DG 24, the consumer affairs directorate, is the newest and weakest of the DGs, while BEUC, the European consumer lobby, is punier and less effective than comparable industrial lobbies. And when reforms of the CAP—a policy which according to some estimates raises the price of food by 15 per cent across the EU—are discussed, consumer voices are seldom heard.

In July 1998 the European Court of Justice ruled that retailers could not sell trademarked goods from outside the EU, such as Levi jeans, without the manufacturers' permission. The companies making such trademarked goods had refused to sell them to supermarkets because they want to control distribution through retailers who agree to charge high prices. So supermarkets had resorted to buying trademarked goods indirectly, on the "grey market". When the Court of Justice ruled this illegal hardly anyone except for a few British supermarkets complained.

Long ago Napoleon observed the shop-centred nature of the British people. The rest of the continent, very slowly, is becoming more consumer conscious. Britain could take the lead in raising that consciousness, for example by campaigning for a directive that would prevent EU rules on selective distribution practices—which keep the price of cars as well as the price of jeans artificially high—from harming the consumer. Any legislation that led to lower prices would help the Union's image by delivering tangible benefits to European citizens.

Europe will not reap the full benefits of its market unless everyone keeps to the rules. The Commission has rightly stepped up its efforts to police the market against governments and companies which abuse it, and could do more. The vitality of the single market depends on a strong Commission. British politicians should be wary of those on the continent who call for the Commission's wings to be clipped: Chancellor Kohl's recent attacks on the Commission have been driven not by an abandonment of his belief in a federal Europe, but by German annoyance that DG 4 has outlawed anti-competitive mergers and state aid.

Another way of strengthening Europe's product markets is to extend them across the Atlantic. In the spring of 1998 Sir Leon Brittan, the trade commissioner, persuaded the Commission to propose a "New Transatlantic Marketplace" (NTM) that would go some way towards creating a single market between the EU and the USA. The scheme would remove technical barriers to trade through mutual recognition or harmonisation of product standards; eliminate industrial tariffs by 2010; create free trade in services; and further liberalise rules on investment, public procurement and intellectual property.

France, however, vetoed discussion of the NTM. Despite the Commission having deliberately excluded agriculture and cultural industries from its proposals, in an effort to assuage French sensibilities, France appeared to fear that the NTM could lead to America having a say in Europe's single market.

In the long run the EU and the United States are bound to pursue something along the lines of the NTM proposals, because each has a clear economic interest in doing so. One should not assume that the French will always have a government that is blind to the economic interests of France. The British government, with both free-trading credentials and excellent connections in Washington, is ideally-placed to revive the plan, as soon as the political situation on both sides of the Atlantic is favourable.

Economic reform should apply not only to labour and to product markets but also to capital markets. Europe's companies would benefit if its variegated capital markets became more united and liquid. The arrival of the euro will speed up this process. The decision of the London and Frankfurt stock exchanges to seek a merger is an encouraging step. But both the EU and national governments need to do more to promote the unification of Europe's capital markets.

Consider the case of Europe's inchoate venture capital markets. One reason why the EU has fewer start-up companies than the United States is that it has many fewer venture capitalists. The EU and American economies are of similar size, yet venture capital investment in the United States is three times higher.

Europe's fragmented markets make it hard for venture capitalists to invest, and for entrepreneurs to raise money outside their home country. For example a prospectus that is valid in one member-state will be invalid in another, while tax and accounting rules vary from country to country. National legislation often prevents institutional investors from putting money into new ventures. Governments usually tax foreign dividends at a higher rate than domestic dividends. And when a European venture capitalist wishes to cash in his or her investment with a flotation, there is no large and liquid pan-European exchange, specialising in the shares of new companies, that is comparable to America's NASDAQ.

Venture capital in Britain is more developed than other EU countries. But in Britain, like the rest of Europe, there is much less investment in higher-risk start-up and high-tech companies than in America; a lot of British venture capital goes into management buy-outs. Nevertheless the fact that the British venture capital market accounts for almost half the Union's total does give Britain an opportunity to offer leadership in this area.

A British government intent on promoting pan-European venture capital would find the European Commission a willing ally. For this is an area of economic reform which requires some action at EU level. Britain should, as a start, support the Commission's proposals for common accounting rules, common prospectuses and an EU-wide regulatory regime for venture capital funds. Later on, the government should be pragmatic in considering the case for EU action in the sensitive area of tax: both the different systems of capital gains tax that apply across the Union, and the differential treatments that governments apply to debt and equity investments impede the development of a pan-European venture capital market.

The government is right to believe that the theme of economic reform could help to re-establish British influence in Europe. The timing is propitious: relatively fast economic growth on the continent makes it easier for governments to embrace reform. To some extent Britain is pushing at an open door. Successive EU summits have endorsed the principles of reform. Many continental governments, such as Spain's, have already done much to liberalise labour markets. And even in France, which remains more resistant to Anglo-Saxon economic philosophy than many parts of the continent, most business leaders understand perfectly well the reforms their country needs; so do some French politicians, but few of them have yet had the courage to say so in public. If British ministers can help to give economic reform a European, rather than a transatlantic pedigree, they will encourage the French and others to embrace it.

Pressing ahead with enlargement

The other great challenge facing the EU, alongside the euro, is enlargement. The Labour government should continue to champion the Union's expansion into Eastern Europe. Several member-states, notably those likely to suffer a sharp loss of EU agricultural funds (such as France) or regional funds (such as Spain) as a consequence of enlargement, are inclined to slow the process. Even countries such as Germany and Austria, which had supported the rapid expansion of the Union in Eastern Europe, have lost their enthusiasm, largely because of worries over free movement of labour. A few years ago it seemed likely that the first East European countries—and the EU has designated the Czech Republic, Estonia, Hungary, Poland and Slovenia as the first wave—would join in about 2002. Now it is likely to be several years later.

Britain should ensure that this process does not grind to a halt. And it should also argue that when countries outside the first wave can meet the requisite democratic, economic and administrative standards, they too should be allowed to start negotiations. Evidently, all the candidate countries still have a lot of work to do before they enter the Union. For example the administrations in several of them are wracked with corruption. Countries cannot be allowed in before they can administer EU rules with a fair degree of efficiency and honesty.

To those who follow European politics closely, the benefits of EU enlargement into Eastern Europe are fairly self-evident. Assuming that the five countries in the first wave of applicants plus Cyprus join, British companies will be able to trade and invest in a single market of 460 million consumers, rather than today's 370 million. And it is clearly desirable that the EU should, through granting membership, strengthen the democratic systems and economic structures of the most eligible East European countries.

But the benefits are not that evident to the wider public which is, understandably, cautious about taking in countries that are so much poorer than the existing members. Enlargement will create losers—such towns that receive less money from EU regional funds, or companies that cannot cope with competition from cheap imports—as well as winners. So the government must make an effort to explain the point of enlargement, lest Eurosceptics focus on the problems it will cause in order to undermine support for the Union as a whole.

Of course, there is nothing new in British governments enthusing over enlargement. Conservative governments wanted a wider Europe in order to make it "shallower": if the EU expanded to 20 or 25 members, they assumed, its institutions—designed originally for a six-member Community—would seize up. Enlargement would dilute the federal aspirations of the founding fathers to such an extent that the EU would end up as little more than a free-trade area.

And the British have always stressed that enlargement is desirable because it will force the EU to downsize the CAP. That argument, though undeniably true, is not the best means of convincing other Europeans to back enlargement. The French, for example—however misguided they may be—regard the CAP as thoroughly desirable and a core policy of the EU.

Some other Europeans are therefore inclined to be cynical about British support for enlargement. The best way of convincing them that the British are genuine enthusiasts is to emphasise—as the government has done during the summer of 1998—that the institutions of an enlarged EU will need radical reform. The government's new-found interest in institutional reform must be sustained.

The kinds of reform that the EU needs in the near future are fairly obvious (some longer-term reforms are considered in the next chapter). The problem of bigger countries such as Britain and France being under-represented in the Council of Ministers, relative to their populations, will worsen, because all the aspirant members bar Poland are small countries. So the large countries should receive more votes but would—in the interests of a more efficient Commission—give up their second commissioner so that each country had just one. The Union should rethink the way it conducts meetings, since the current *tours de table*, with every government speaking in turn, take too long and discourage useful discussion.

Federalist commentators tend to exaggerate the importance of extending qualified majority voting (QMV). Most of the important policy areas that relate to the single market are already subject to QMV. Nevertheless many policy areas in the first pillar still require unanimity and, in order to speed up decision-making, should be considered for transfer to QMV. These include industrial policy, transport regulation, agricultural prices, some environmental matters, culture, competition policy, development aid, the management of the structural funds and trade negotiations for service industries.

The Amsterdam treaty says that decisions on asylum, immigration and frontier controls should switch to QMV five years after the treaty goes into force, if there is then unanimous agreement in favour. Hopefully there will be. But several other areas subject to unanimity will probably have to remain so for the foreseeable future, because of their sensitivity. These include co-ordination of social security systems, citizenship, taxation, the tasks of the ECB, exchange rate policy, budgetary questions, international treaties and changes to the EU treaties.

Institutional discussions tend to be dull and are unlikely to inspire many people to take a greater interest in the EU. But they are also important:

if the EU ignored the institutions while it took in new members it would end up taking decisions less effectively. That would lead to legislation of lower quality, which would not only be bad for business but also fuel popular disenchantment with the EU.

Jean Monnet wrote in his memoirs (published in 1978): "Unlike many people, I never feared that the entry of Great Britain would impair the smooth functioning of the Community. 'They want things to work', I explained, 'and when they see that Europe can only work through its institutions, they will be the strongest defenders of them.'" For much of the past 20 years, the British have failed to live up to Monnet's expectations. But Tony Blair's new-found interest in the future of the EU suggests that Monnet may finally be proved right. Having already shown a radical approach to the British constitution the Labour government now needs to do the same for Europe.

Evidently, enlargement requires much more than institutional reform. It cannot happen without radical reform of the EU budget, the common agricultural policy and the regional funds. The Commission's proposals in these areas—covered in its "Agenda 2000" document—would lower farm prices and focus subsidies on smaller farmers, while constraining the EU budget within its current limit of 1.27 per cent of the Union's GDP. (A detailed examination of the Agenda 2000 package is beyond the scope of this booklet and will be dealt with in future CER publications.) Britain has rightly supported this package of proposals.

The government should press for an agreement on Agenda 2000 during the German presidency in the first half of 1999. If those negotiations become protracted the timetable for enlargement is likely to slip further. Britain should also urge its partners to agree on a deadline of, say, 2004, for the first new members—assuming they can satisfy the required criteria—to join the Union. The history of the EU suggests that deadlines are a useful means of preventing foot-dragging. Choosing dates in advance helped to achieve the customs union by 1970, the single market by the end of 1992 and—it appears—EMU in January 1999.

Pragmatism on justice and home affairs
Most people assume that monetary union will be the principal force behind future European integration. But while the euro may well lead to

much greater co-ordination of economic policy, co-operation on justice and home affairs (JHA) could rival, or possibly surpass EMU as a growth area for EU activity. Already, about a third of the paperwork passing through the UK representation in Brussels concerns JHA. So it is hard for Britain to claim that it can lead in Europe when it has opted out of not only EMU but also a large part of JHA co-operation.

The EU's commitment to the free movement of people within its borders obliges interior ministries to work together. The abolition of internal frontiers—already implemented by most member-states—requires a common approach to visas, asylum and external frontiers. And it makes it highly desirable for police forces and judicial systems to co-operate. Britain and Ireland (the latter because it wants to maintain its own passport union with Britain) have opted out of the scrapping of the EU's internal frontier controls. But they have a strong interest in what happens at its external frontier, since that affects who turns up at their ports and airports.

The Maastricht treaty placed almost all JHA co-operation in a "third pillar", in which the Council of Ministers takes decisions by unanimity, the Commission and Parliament have only minimal roles and the Court of Justice has no role at all. Progress in this area has been slow. The institutional arrangements of the third pillar are widely regarded as ineffective. No single body has the sole right of initiative or the expertise to drive forward the agenda. There is a shortage of suitable legal instruments for establishing formal co-operation: one of the more powerful instruments available, the convention, is effectively an international treaty and cannot apply until ratified by every signatory, which may take years. Furthermore, the exclusion of the Court means that there is no means of ensuring that member-states fulfil their obligations.

Institutional weaknesses explain only some of the lack of achievement. Until recently interior ministries had very little experience of working together. Ministers and officials have needed time to get to know each other. And it does seem that when a group of countries has enough political will—as with the British presidency's insistence, strongly supported by Belgium, that something be done to combat paedophile crime—measures can be pushed through quite fast.

The 1997 Amsterdam treaty, which is not expected to enter into force until early in 1999, shifts JHA areas that relate to freedom of movement into the "first" pillar, that of normal EU business. Thus conventional EU procedures, including (after a five-year delay) the Commission having the sole right of initiative, will apply to external border controls, asylum and immigration rules. Britain and Ireland have opted out of these areas but are included in discussions and have the right to participate in any policies that are agreed—subject to the approval of the other member-states. Judicial co-operation on civil matters is also within the first pillar, while police work and judicial co-operation on criminal cases are still covered by the inter-governmental arrangements of the third pillar.

In Britain these Home Office dossiers are extremely sensitive politically. British governments of left and right have never seriously considered scrapping passport controls, partly because they fear Eurosceptics would rail against the prospect of hordes of foreigners infiltrating Britain's shores, but also because the policy makes some sense for an island surrounded by cold water. Most other member-states have long land borders that are impractical to patrol, and therefore require everyone to carry identity cards. The Home Office argues that since nearly all visitors enter Britain via a small number of airports, seaports and the Channel tunnel, it is more effective to carry out external border checks than to rely on internal controls. Any British government which ended frontier controls would almost certainly introduce identity cards in their place, a prospect that would horrify many Britons. Furthermore, Britain's relatively harmonious race relations could be strained by impromptu identity checks, as any Parisian of North African origin will testify.

But Britain's refusal to give up border controls, however understandable, carries a price. The government will find it harder to push other member-states to enforce the EU's external frontier controls strictly. And the recent arrival in Dover of Slovak gypsies—hundreds of whom had passed unchecked through several EU countries—shows that the rest of the Union's decisions on internal and external borders have consequences for Britain.

The enlargement of the Union is likely to worsen the problem of illegal immigration and international criminal networks—many of which emanate from the former Soviet Union—unless applicant countries can strengthen external border controls and improve their customs and police capabilities. These countries are not getting enough financial and technical assistance to help them prepare. But having opted out of the common external frontier, Britain is in a weak position to urge its partners to give more assistance to the East European states.

Britain's broad objective of becoming a more influential member of the Union requires a more constructive approach to JHA. It should be possible for Britain to retain passport controls and yet pursue more positive policies in other areas. Britain could then more easily urge its partners to strengthen, where necessary, their own stretches of the EU's external frontier.

First, Britain should view the free movement policies of the first pillar with a pragmatic spirit. Britain has a strong interest in opting in to asylum policy. For if the others adopted a more restrictive common policy than Britain, asylum seekers would flock to its shores. Another reason for involvement in a common policy is to try and prevent member-states from competing against each other to impose ever-tighter restrictions on asylum seekers, to the detriment of their rights.

Second, the government should keep up the efforts it is already making to encourage practical co-operation among police forces and customs authorities. Fortunately, Britain has not opted out of the third pillar and so is an equal partner in these areas. Britain's reputation for administrative efficiency and the relative competence of its police and customs services place it in a strong position. It also helps that the Home Office is—to the surprise of many—becoming an unexpected source of creative thinking on matters European.

The convention establishing Europol was finally ratified in May 1998, thanks in part to chivvying by the British presidency. When Europol is fully established it could be an important tool in the fight against terrorism, organised crime, fraud and the trafficking of young women, children and drugs. Europol's main role will be to act as a network for exchanging criminal intelligence. It has already been operating in embryonic form as the European Drugs Unit, of which Britain has made good use. No country, except possibly Germany, wants to turn Europol into a European FBI that could pursue and arrest criminals, but Britain should keep an open mind on increasing its resources and operational capacity.

Third, and most controversially, Britain could press for progress on the mutual recognition of criminal justice systems. Anyone who commits a murder in Britain can be fairly sure that if he flees to the continent he will be pursued. But that is often not the case with less serious crimes. There is little need to harmonise laws or judicial procedures, for much progress could be made through the mutual recognition of court decisions and of warrants for arrest. For example, if a French court fined a Briton, a British court could enforce payment. It would also be useful if one country's authorities could collect evidence more easily in another, particularly against financial fraudsters, for example through wire taps.

Consider how progress in these areas could have affected the case of Kenneth Noye, wanted for murder in Britain and apprehended in Spain in August 1998. The British government had to start complex and lengthy extradition procedures which were likely to take many weeks. If JHA co-operation had managed to simplify extradition procedures there would have been less delay; and if that co-operation had gone as far as mutual recognition of warrants for arrest, Noye could have been whisked back to Britain instantly.

Evidently, the government will need to tread carefully in such a politically sensitive area as law and order. But most Britons understand that a lot of crime has an international dimension. The government should highlight the EU's work in these areas, rather than be fearful of admitting it, for such co-operation shows that the Union can deliver tangible benefits.

Strengthening foreign policy

Foreign policy is a British strength. The quality of its diplomatic service, like that of its armed forces, is envied throughout the world. The government should make a point of explaining to the British people that, in many parts of the world, Britain can achieve more through working with its EU partners than on its own. But the European Union's current methods for co-ordinating foreign policy do not work well, so the British government should push to make them more effective.

Many will regard that goal with great cynicism. After all, the Union failed to agree on a united response to the crisis over Iraq early in 1998. Nevertheless most of the Europeans' fundamental foreign policy interests are similar, most of the time. There has, for example, been a common policy to enlarge the Union into Eastern Europe, and to deepen ties of trade and aid, as well as political contacts, with all applicants, including those that are unlikely to join in the foreseeable future.

European nations share common values of democracy, human rights, social justice, market economics, internationalism and concern for the environment. Much of the civilised world shares these values, of course. But Europeans tend to be more concerned than Americans to support multinational negotiations and the rule of international law. Thus America refused to sign the treaty establishing the International Criminal Court in the Hague, in July 1998. When a united EU succeeds in projecting its values into the global arena it can be a force for good: at the Kyoto summit on global warming, in November 1997, the EU took the lead in brokering an agreement to cut greenhouse gas emissions.

In 1998 the EU's attempts to stop Kosovo sliding towards war are proving no more effective than earlier efforts to prevent war in Bosnia. But the Europeans and the United States have at least agreed on the principal ingredients of a peaceful settlement: Serbia should withdraw its forces from Kosovo, the Kosovars—including the Kosovo Liberation Army— should form a united front that would be prepared to negotiate and Kosovo should become an autonomous unit within Yugoslavia.

In the Middle East the EU countries have somewhat different foreign policy interests to the United States. Robin Cook's visit to the Har Homa settlement in March 1998 made the point that, as far as the EU is concerned, Israel's insistence on building new settlements on the West Bank is gravely damaging the to Arab-Israeli peace process. The Israeli and Thatcherite media pilloried Mr Cook for having upset Binyamin Netanyahu, the Israeli prime minister, by visiting the settlement. Some aspects of Mr Cook's itinerary could have been handled more sensitively, but his visit did much to salvage the reputation of the British presidency in Arab countries and in continental capitals. The EU brings its own perspective, one that is less reluctant to criticise Israeli policies, to the Middle East peace process. It therefore has a legitimate, useful and complementary role to play as a partner, if a junior one, to the Americans.

Perhaps the biggest test for European foreign policy is the Turkey-Cyprus conundrum. Relations between the EU and Turkey have almost broken down. The Turks are still smarting from having been left in a category all by themselves, behind 11 other would-be members, at the December 1997 Luxembourg summit. And the start of membership talks between the EU and Cyprus has maddened the Turks. If the southern part of Cyprus joins the EU, they say, they will annex Turkish-run northern Cyprus. But Greece says that if southern Cyprus is not allowed into the EU it will veto the applications of the East Europeans.

Meanwhile there is a chance of war breaking out in Cyprus, where a Turkish Cypriot boycott has brought talks between the island's two communities to a halt. The Cypriot government has delayed but not cancelled an order for Russian S-300 anti-aircraft missiles. Turkey promises that if the missiles arrive it will attack the installations, while Greece is bound by military agreements to defend Cyprus from attack.

The EU states have an evident common interest in sorting out the Cyprus problem—though the fact that one of their own number, Greece, is a protagonist, and has vetoed all EU financial aid to Turkey for more than a decade, makes it harder for them to act. The Americans, of course, are also concerned to prevent a conflict between two NATO allies. But their perspective is principally geostrategic, focused on Turkey's importance for the stability of the Middle East. Thus when Americans call, as they often do, for the EU countries to let in Turkey soon, they overlook problems which matter to Europeans, such as Turkey's backward economy, its refusal to search for political solutions to the Kurdish insurrection and the prominent role of the armed forces in the country's political life.[7]

[7] See David Barchard, "Turkey and the European Union", CER, 1998; and Dan Bilefsky and Charles Grant, "Trouble in the Med", World Link, July/August 1998

Britain is well-placed to help its European partners and the Americans to unravel these knots. As the former colonial power in Cyprus, it has some knowledge of the island. And unlike a country such as Germany, which has a serious problem in its bilateral relations with Turkey, Britain is not particularly close to or hostile to either Greece or Turkey. Sir David Hannay, a British diplomat who is the EU's special envoy on Cyprus, has worked hard to prepare the ground for a settlement.

A European initiative should involve the following elements: Cyprus would cancel its order of Russian missiles; all parties would agree to the demilitarisation of Cypriot air space; the Turkish Cypriots would join the Greek Cypriots in negotiating both entry into the Union and a federal constitution for Cyprus; the EU would arrange a special programme of economic assistance for Northern Cyprus; Greece would unblock financial aid that the EU has long promised to Turkey; the EU would assure Turkey that it will be able to join the club when it meets the many criteria that it does not currently meet; and the Turkish government would admit that it has to work hard in order to make the grade for membership.

The major impediment to more coherent and effective European foreign policies has undoubtedly been the lack of political will among the 15 governments. But institutional arrangements can, at the margin, make a difference. The current Common Foreign and Security Policy (CFSP) machinery does not work well: the presidency rotates from country to country every six months; a "troika" of foreign ministers from the past, present and future presidencies represents the Union; a small secretariat within the Council of Ministers attempts to co-ordinate policy; and the Commission, which takes the lead on the economic side of foreign policy, is kept at arm's length.

The Amsterdam treaty contains some promising ideas for improving these arrangements. It introduces majority voting for decisions concerning the implementation of agreed policies; a procedure for "constructive abstention", so that a country can dissociate itself from a decision rather than veto it; a central policy-planning unit, to encourage EU foreign ministers to develop common analyses; and the post of a "high representative" for foreign policy—known as "Mr CFSP"—to act as spokesman for the EU.

Britain and France, as the EU members with the most experienced diplomatic corps, are ideally suited to guide the implementation of these reforms. Tony Blair seems to have taken this point on board. Speaking in the Hague on 20 January, just before the Iraqi crisis became serious, he said: "On external policy the EU must be both effective and seen to be effective internationally...We must equip Europe with better machinery. This means the right candidate to be the EU's voice on common foreign and security policy issues, and the right back-up."

Some EU foreign ministers, jealous of their own power, are calling for "Mr CFSP" to be a mere official. But in order to be effective the high representative will need to be able to stand up to the foreign ministers and argue for the common interest. He or she should provide the continuity that the rotating presidency cannot deliver, and would have to work closely with the Commission. If the office proves a success it could gradually take on some of the foreign policy tasks of the rotating presidency, such as chairing meetings of foreign ministers.[8]

[8] See Charles Grant, "Strength in Numbers: Europe's foreign and defence policy", CER, 1996

Britain should push for a political heavyweight, of the stature of, say, Chris Patten (the former Hong Kong governor), Carl Bildt (the former EU envoy in Bosnia) or Volker Rühe (the German defence minister) to take on the job. Such a figure would at last provide an answer to the problem Henry Kissinger stated in the early 1970s: when he wanted to speak to Europe he did not know whom to call. EU governments worry that a high representative with clout could pursue his own agenda and rival their authority. But so long as they choose a tactful person who understands the sensitivities of his position that need not be a problem; he will work under the instructions of the foreign ministers, and be answerable to them, in the way that NATO's secretary-general is to NATO foreign ministers.

Britain should consider further reforms. The EU's political committee, which consists of the "political directors" (senior officials from each foreign ministry), is supposed to steer EU foreign policy at the level below the foreign ministers. But the political directors, who meet twice a month, usually keep to already-formed national positions and seldom engage in meaningful discussions of policy. The political committee should be based permanently in Brussels, on a par with the "Coreper" committee of permanent representatives to the EU. If it met more frequently, under the chairmanship of Mr CFSP, and spent more time talking to the Commission and other EU bodies, it might make a more useful contribution.

For the Labour government, improving the EU's diplomatic co-ordination would be a low-risk enterprise. The institutional machinery would be within the Council of Ministers, meaning that governments, rather than the Commission would be in the driving seat. And since important decisions on foreign policy require unanimity, nobody need fret about ceding sovereignty. Such improvements would be applauded elsewhere in the world. The Clinton administration, for example, would be delighted if the EU could react more quickly and speak with a more unified voice.

Redesigning European defence

Defence is another potential British strength. Britain and France are
the only European countries capable of projecting power beyond
Europe. Germany has relaxed its rule of never sending troops outside
the NATO area by contributing to the peacekeeping forces in Bosnia.
But its armed forces, dependent on conscripts and heavily geared to
territorial defence, remain less capable than those of Britain or France.
And they still cannot serve outside the NATO area except when covered
by a UN mandate.

Yet defence is also a potential British weakness. For Britain's longstanding
hostility to the concept of European defence, and its tendency to line up
beside the Americans within NATO, only confirms, to many continentals,
that its destiny lies across the Atlantic rather than in Europe.

However, in the 1991 Maastricht treaty Britain did accept the principle
of "the eventual framing of a common defence policy, which might in time
lead to a common defence" for the European Union. And in June 1996,
at a NATO meeting in Berlin, Britain and the United States both accepted
the idea of a European defence identity within NATO. The 16 NATO
nations agreed that, when America did not want to involve its forces in
a mission, European officers in NATO's command structure could detach
themselves and reconfigure as a European-only command, to manage
task forces of European troops. The Western European Union, an
independent organisation that acts as the EU's defence wing (but in which
the four EU neutral countries and Denmark do not participate) would run
such European-only missions.

France's decision in 1997 not to rejoin NATO's military structure, as it
had intended—because of a Franco-American row over whether a
European or an American should command NATO's southern
headquarters at Naples—has for the time being stymied the development
of this European identity within NATO.

The Berlin accords revealed that, in practice, most EU governments accept
that NATO is the only European defence organisation that can be
effective in the foreseeable future. But at a symbolic level, France,
Germany and others continued to hanker after a more purely European
defence entity. In the negotiation of the 1997 Treaty of Amsterdam, like

that of Maastricht before it, France and Germany pushed for the long-term prospect of the WEU merging with the EU.

The British opposed such a merger. They have always feared that any attempt to boost Europe's defence identity, either through a stronger WEU or the EU itself, could impair NATO's military effectiveness, or needlessly duplicate its functions, or annoy the Americans and so hasten their departure from Europe. The British found allies among the EU's neutrals—Austria, Ireland, Finland and Sweden—which did not want the Union to grow military wings.

In March 1997, when Albania degenerated into anarchy, and European governments discussed a military mission to quell the disorder, Britain joined Germany in vetoing the use of the WEU. Britain took that position because it did not want to send troops and thought the mission would be ineffective, but also because , "theologically", it did not wish to boost the importance of the WEU. In the event the Italians led a European task force which made a useful contribution to the restoration of order in Albania.

A few months later the Amsterdam treaty defined the content of the Union's common defence policy to include "humanitarian and rescue tasks, peacekeeping tasks and tasks of combat forces in crisis management, including peacemaking". The Union can "avail itself of the WEU" to carry out these tasks, while EU members not in the WEU may join in such missions.

Post-Amsterdam, however, Europe's security architecture remains an unsatisfactory mess. The WEU is still an organisation in search of a role, sitting uneasily between NATO and the European Union. The French remain semi-detached from NATO. And the EU's nascent common foreign policy is weakened by its disconnection from any military organisation that could support its positions.

This situation offers opportunities to a Britain that is keen to be more influential in Europe. In the spring of 1998 Mr Blair began to talk of Britain taking a lead on European defence. He may have realised that, if the British could appear to be better Europeans in this area, they might win considerable credit with their partners; and that in the strange world of EU politics, it is possible to buy good will by making concessions that are more symbolic than substantial.

What Britain needs to do is find ways of strengthening European defence without damaging NATO or upsetting the Americans. First, it should continue the good progress it has made on deepening bilateral military relationships with its European allies, particularly the French. The British and French armies have for the most part worked well together in Bosnia. But both the British and French governments have always said that, if America withdraws from the NATO-led peacekeeping force there, they will withdraw too. They should have the courage to declare that they would like the Americans to stay, but that if the US pulls out ground troops France and Britain are capable of leading the peacekeeping force in Bosnia.

Whether the resultant force was called NATO or WEU or EU is not material; it would certainly depend on NATO—meaning to a large extent American—assets. Militarily, however, American ground troops are not needed in Bosnia (in fact they currently contribute rather little, the Pentagon being so reluctant to put them in harm's way). Politically, such a British-French *démarche* would greatly increase American respect for the EU.

Second, the British should try to broker a compromise between the Americans and the French on the latter's reintegration into NATO's command structure. So long as the French remain outside, the alliance is militarily and politically weaker, and its European identity cannot come to much. In the argument over the Naples command, both France and the United States have been guilty of stubborn and inept diplomacy. Given that Britain has some influence in the American defence establishment, it is well placed to help find a solution.

Third, Britain should not flag in its efforts lead the restructuring of the European defence industry. Mr Blair has already devoted considerable energy to this, persuading Messrs Kohl, Chirac and Jospin to sign a statement in December 1997 that called upon Europe's defence companies to come up with a plan for consolidation. It is not Mr Blair's fault that this plan's ambitions have yet to be realised. The French government has held up the creation of a military aircraft company along the lines of

Airbus by refusing to accept the full privatisation of Aérospatiale. British Aerospace and Daimler-Benz Aerospace remain reluctant to merge with Aérospatiale because they want the new company to be run on commercial principles.

The French will probably not fully privatise Aérospatiale, or push a reluctant Dassault into cross-border restructuring, unless they believe that the British and German aerospace industries are about to merge without them. The British and the Germans must therefore be prepared to call France's bluff. Britain also has a crucial role to play in ensuring that the European defence industry does not cut itself off from that in America. Technologically, American defence companies are now far ahead of those in Europe. Therefore the European firms, while rationalising among themselves, need to remain open to alliances with those in America. If they shut themselves off from American technology they are doomed to decline.

Finally, Britain should propose abolishing the WEU. Its political functions would merge with the European Union, becoming a "fourth pillar" (after the European Community, pillar one, the CFSP, pillar two, and justice and home affairs, pillar three). Its military functions would be subsumed into NATO. Article five of the WEU treaty, obliging members to defend each other from attack, and enforceable only through NATO, would be transferred to the fourth pillar.

The point of assigning the EU's military role to a fourth pillar, rather than the second, is that not all member-states want to take part in common defence policies, while all are in the CFSP. Just as Britain and Denmark have been allowed to opt out of EMU, Austria, Finland, Ireland, Sweden and Denmark would not join the fourth pillar. As the EU enlarged, some East European countries might not want to join the fourth pillar. Indeed countries not in NATO could not join it, or they would be gaining a security guarantee without contributing anything to collective defence.

French diplomats argue that the WEU should be merged with the second pillar, on the grounds that the CFSP would be more effective if its political and military components were part of a single organisation. In practice there would probably not be much difference between this French scheme, under which neutral and non-NATO countries would have to opt out of the second pillar's defence organisation, and this booklet's proposal for a fourth pillar.

European defence ministers should meet as an EU council. They could instruct NATO's European forces to take part in EU military missions. The mechanism for European-only task forces was agreed at NATO's 1996 Berlin meeting. The presumption would be that the United States would not veto the use of NATO assets in support of these European missions. It made that promise in Berlin. The Europeans' use of NATO assets is evidently a potential source of argument, though the Americans would have a strong incentive to oblige: if they said no the Europeans would think seriously about organising their defence outside NATO.

Such EU missions would be relatively modest. If the military task required a massive use of air power, heavy armour, information-gathering capacity and so on, the Americans would almost certainly want to be involved and the Europeans would probably not want to act on their own.

The reconstruction of Europe's defence architecture along the lines proposed in this booklet would bring several benefits:

★ The WEU, an organisation that—despite an able secretary-general, José Cutileiro—is going nowhere, would be put out of its misery; it cannot develop further without starting to duplicate NATO's functions, which nobody wants.

★ The CFSP would be strengthened: if the EU was able to call on military assets, is pronouncements on foreign policy would carry more clout. The likes of Slobodan Milosevic might listen with more respect.

★ These reforms, by finally settling the question of Europe's defence identity, should convince everyone that NATO has a future as Europe's only functioning military organisation. And that should help to maintain America's military commitment to Europe.

★ Establishing a fourth pillar would make it easier for the EU to admit countries unwilling or unable to join a defence organisation, thereby ensuring that Europe's emerging defence identity did not slow down enlargement. French thinking, which tends to assume that the EU's neutral members and future new members should in the long run participate fully in European defence, could slow enlargement. In any case, Russia is less likely to take exception to EU enlargement (which it has so far accepted without complaint) if it can see that the military guarantee does not apply to all members and that—as is likely on current scenarios—the Baltic republics would not join the fourth pillar.

These ideas are far from being adopted as British policy, but have been mooted in the Foreign Office and the Ministry of Defence. How would Britain's partners react? There is a reasonable chance that they would agree to this scheme, if only because it offers something to each of the principal countries. France and Germany would fulfil their long-standing objective of merging the WEU and the EU, while America would see the European defence identity emerging within a stronger NATO rather than as a rival to it.

Some Americans do have reservations about this scheme, for it would inevitably lead to a European caucus within NATO. And that might prove bothersome to the United States. The EU countries could turn up to a NATO meeting unwilling—or unable—to renegotiate their common position. Other Americans worry that an EU with a defence capability could be dragged into a military conflict and then expect the Americans to rescue it. Suppose that an EU member in neither NATO nor the fourth pillar, such as Estonia, reckoning that EU membership offered an implicit security guarantee, provoked a war that soon involved the entire Union. The answer to this worry is to stress that an EU security guarantee would depend on NATO membership and that the EU would have neither the will nor the means to embark on a major military enterprise without American support.

Despite such concerns, many American strategists, including top Pentagon officials and even senior advisers to Jesse Helms, the right-wing Republican who chairs the Senate Foreign Relations Committee, are prepared to support the ideas outlined in this paper. They believe that a European caucus within NATO is a price worth paying for a scheme which offers the prospect of a more coherent European CFSP, and of a stronger and longer-lasting NATO. Meanwhile a forthcoming report on transatlantic relations from the Aspen Institute, Berlin, signed by security experts from Britain, the Czech Republic, France, Germany, Norway, Poland and the United States endorses this plan for European defence.

5 Confronting the democratic deficit

Europe's elusive demos

The European Union, for many people, is a distant, incomprehensible, overweening and thoroughly unappealing entity. The wave of Euroscepticism which ran over much of northern Europe in the early 1990s has yet to subside. There is scant popular support for the federalist vision of the EU's founding fathers, yet the current set of European leaders has failed to make the case for a credible or coherent alternative.

The coming of the euro, bringing with it a hugely powerful but unelected European Central Bank, will make the Union seem even more undemocratic. It is true that national governments, Britain included, have already delegated monetary authority to independent central banks. But the Bank of England is run by Britons for the benefit of Britons and operates in a political context with which most Britons are familiar. Eurosceptics will miss no opportunity to point out that the ECB is run by foreigners for the benefit of foreigners and that it is part of an alien political system.

If, as is likely, Ecofin and/or the Euro-11 Committee take on an important role in co-ordinating economic policies, the democratic deficit is likely to loom even larger. Of course finance ministers, unlike members of the ECB council, are elected politicians; but when they meet in Brussels, as part of a body that is evidently powerful but whose role is hard to fathom, they seem remote.

Thus a central element of the Britain's European strategy must be to help the EU find new ways of reconnecting to the people. There is no point in British ministers becoming influential in Brussels if their work is stymied by popular revolts against the EU in Britain and elsewhere. Britain, with its strong parliamentary and democratic traditions, is well placed to play a major role in tackling the widespread dissatisfaction with the Union. And since Britain hosts a potent current of Euroscepticism, its politicians have a better idea than some of just how unattractive the EU can appear.

The roots of this popular antipathy to the Union lie in the mid-1980s, when the combination of the single market programme and the Single European Act (which introduced qualified majority voting for single market laws) boosted its powers. The dismantling of non-tariff barriers to trade and the regulation of state aid and mergers meant that some companies relocated and some people lost jobs. And then in 1991 the Maastricht treaty, with its plan for a single currency, promised to touch an essential element of sovereignty. So it was perhaps natural that many people would resent what seemed to be an arrogant and increasingly powerful bureaucracy in Brussels.

The Union's institutions have little legitimacy in the eyes of many Europeans. The poor image of the European Commission, the embodiment of "Brussels", derives partly from its tendency, in the late 1980s and early 1990s, to regulate in too much detail and to grab more power for itself. A more fundamental difficulty is that commissioners are appointed by governments rather than elected. Yet even the European Parliament, directly elected since 1979, has failed to win much credibility: at each successive European election, a smaller proportion of the electorate has bothered to vote.

The EU's problem is partly geographical: Brussels is inevitably more distant than the national governments with which people can readily identify (for similar reasons the US government in Washington DC is mistrusted more than state governments). But the EU creates its own special problems of legitimacy. As Raymond Aron wrote: "The European idea is empty...it was created by intellectuals, and that fact accounts for its genuine appeal to the mind and its feeble appeal to the heart." [9]

[9] *Raymond Aron, "The century of total war", Doubleday, 1954*

The EU is a political system that does not correspond to the kind of social and cultural reality with which many EU citizens can readily identify. The "community of interest" that ties together, say, Germans and Greeks is already stretched pretty thin; enlargement of the Union into Eastern Europe will make it thinner still. How many Germans will want to pay taxes that are recycled as regional aid to Romania?

Mark Leonard expresses the problem thus:

> *The holy grail of legitimacy seekers is a shared sense of identity and destiny. It short-circuits the entire debate about whether an institution should exist, as people will unconditionally support the existence of an entity to which they see themselves belonging. It is identity that allows governments to take "tough decisions" or bring about major change. It is what carries political systems through the bad times as well as the good."[10]*

[10] *Mark Leonard, "Europa: the search for European identity", Demos, 1998*

According to figures cited in this Demos pamphlet, 45 per cent of Europeans identify with their nationality but not at all with Europe; 40 per cent identify first with their nationality and second with Europe; and just over ten per cent feel European first. Leonard makes much of the absence of unifying myths and stories of the sort that would, in a nation, contribute to a sense of identity, and the fact that more than half of Europeans are incapable of having a conversation in a second language.

When Jacques Delors became European Commission president, in 1985, he attempted to give the EU some of the trappings of statehood: the *Ode to joy* theme of Beethoven's 9th symphony became the EU anthem; the 12 yellow stars were borrowed from the Council of Europe, to become the EU flag; maroon EU passports and bodies such as the European Union Youth Orchestra emerged. And then in 1991, during the negotiation of the Maastricht treaty, Felipe González, Spain's prime minister, invented the idea of EU citizenship. The treaty gave EU citizens the right to vote in, or be elected in the local or European elections of countries other than their own, and the right to call on other countries' consular services. Evidently, none of these attempts to create a feeling of common identity has had much impact on most ordinary Europeans.

Yet the problem may not be quite as extreme as Mr Leonard suggests. After all, Europeans do share a common, bloody and inter-mingled history. Most of them are aware that the EU makes another war among its members inconceivable. And they know that a whole host of problems, for example pollution, drug trafficking or war in the Balkans are better tackled through the European countries working together. As for the supposed absence of a common culture, even some of the more Eurosceptical Britons will admit, after a visit to the United States, or South East Asia, or the Middle East, that they feel thoroughly European.

Mr Leonard's two recent pamphlets on the EU say virtually nothing about economics.[11] The average Londoner may not feel that the average inhabitant of Munich, or indeed Bucharest, is his kith and kin. But he may well have an instinctive understanding of the economic benefits of being part of a transnational market. The British Social Attitudes Survey, 1997, reported that 67 per cent of Britons welcome the freedom to get jobs in other EU countries, while 77 per cent think it important that the UK can sell goods in EU countries without customs duties.

11 The second, "Rediscovering Europe", also published by Demos in 1998, builds on the work begun in "Europa: the search for European identity."

Since Britain joined the European Union an increasing proportion of its trade, as well as foreign direct investment (both in and out) has been with the continent. The EU took 57 per cent of British visible exports in 1997, while the whole of Asia and the Middle East took just 15 per cent (including invisibles, the EU took 49 per cent of British exports in 1997). The proportion of foreign direct investment in Britain from EU countries has risen to about 30 per cent. Those whose jobs depend on these flows are more likely to think the EU a worthwhile enterprise.

Increasing economic, but also social and cultural integration may eventually rub off on popular attitudes. Labour mobility is greater than many people imagine. The last census, in 1991, recorded just over half a million people living in Britain who had been born in other EU countries (not counting 600,000 people from the Irish republic), since when the numbers, at least in London, appear to have increased substantially. Industrial lobbies, trade unions and non-governmental organisations are becoming ever more intertwined in pan-European alliances.

Youth cultures, in eastern as well as western Europe, have tended to converge on similar sorts of music, fashion and lifestyle. The fact that some of this common culture is American does not make it any less of a unifying force within Europe. In any case the English language, rapidly becoming Europe's lingua franca, is doing more than EU directives—or American cultural icons—to bring young people together. Several EU programmes help: "Erasmus" allows 85,000 students a year to study in countries other than their own.

Every survey of British views on Europe finds that younger people are the most positive. One of the most extensive surveys, for the 1996 British Social Attitudes, concluded that "the young, graduates and the salariat are more likely than average to be in favour of integration. For example, nearly half of those with degree level qualifications are pro-integration—compared with less than a fifth of those without such qualifications."

Of course, Britons who feel a cultural affinity with those across the Channel do not necessarily warm to the lacklustre institutions of Brussels. But while these Britons may condemn the institutions for their irrelevance or poor performance, they would be less likely to do so out of visceral xenophobia. They may at least be open to argument about the worth of the EU, if presented with a convincing case.

Thus there is, perhaps, the beginnings of a European demos, at least for the younger, the better educated and the more affluent. But Europhiles should not suppose that all they have to do is wait for the older generation to fade away, for university education to expand and for the middle classes to grow. For many years to come, cosmopolitan users of inter-rail or the internet will be in a minority. The challenge for pro-Europeans is to explain the EU's relevance to the many poor, ill-educated Britons who do not travel and who fear for their future. They were the sort of people who, in September 1992, almost swung the French referendum against the Maastricht treaty. In a future British referendum, such people could scupper plans to join the euro.

Subsidiarity and transparency

How can the British government, and the others, try to reduce popular disdain for the Brussels institutions? There is no simple, easy answer to the problem of the EU's remoteness. So it is important that the EU handles only those policies which cannot be better dealt with at national or regional level—that is, it should practice subsidiarity. Every few years someone suggests trying to define subsidiarity by stipulating the tasks that need to be performed by the EU, those that it should share with the member-states and those which it should leave entirely to them.

But such efforts never succeed. One problem is that while there are few fields in which the EU has exclusive competence, such as foreign trade and agriculture, there are very many in which competence is and should be shared, for example competition policy, the environment and regional aid. And even in some of the areas where member-states take all the important decisions, such as health and education, the Commission has a minor role—for example in AIDS awareness programmes and educational exchanges.

The trouble with subsidiarity is that it is a very subjective concept. One country's unnecessary interference from Brussels is another country's desire for the EU to impose decent, civilised standards. Thus the Germans have often favoured detailed EU rules on the ingredients allowed in beer, though Britain and other countries see no rationale for EU involvement. But during the recent British presidency Jacques Santer, the Commission president, accused Britain of ignoring subsidiarity when it insisted on pushing ahead with a directive on the condition of animals in zoos.

It is often the directives or policies that most obviously breach subsidiarity which are the most popular. Thus a strict application of the principle might lead to a lesser EU role in those parts of environmental regulation—such as purity of drinking water and bathing water—that do not have a cross-border element. Yet the EU's efforts to clean up beaches have, through delivering a visible benefit, proved extremely popular. Several EU directives on employee rights—such as those on information and consultation, and working time—are not strictly necessary for the smooth working of the market; but they are popular, even in Eurosceptical Britain, and their repeal would diminish support for the Union among many working people.

In practice it is hard to find many centrally-managed tasks that could be devolved to member-states without either causing great annoyance to some governments and some sections of public opinion, or serious inefficiencies. The recent directive that bans tobacco advertising, for example, is a clear breach of subsidiarity. But scrapping it would vex the majority of EU governments that voted for it.

In most of the areas in which the EU is involved it will continue to work with the member-states, and the balance between their roles will remain a question for delicate political judgement. In any case, the arrival of the euro, which will centralise monetary policy and perhaps some fiscal policy, is likely to give EU instutions more rather than less to do.

But there may be ways of reassuring those who fear the increasing concentration of power in Brussels. The Foreign Office's recent thinking on the future of the EU came up with the powerful idea that, in areas which do not require detailed regulation, a more devolved approach to policy-making could become the norm. The Council of Ministers would set broad targets and a timetable for action, leaving each government the discretion to decide how to meet those targets. "In many...areas we should focus on setting standards rather than on imposing directives," said Robin Cook in August.[12]

[12] Interview by John Lloyd, New Statesman, 14.8.98

That is how the Union is tackling unemployment: it provides a framework in which governments can learn from the best practice of others and, influenced by peer-group pressure, adopt new policies (see page 28). The potential benefits of this method are evident: agreement on objectives can be reached relatively fast; national political sensitivities are respected; and governments are more likely to adopt policies that can be seen to be working successfully elsewhere.

A similar approach is already emerging in several policy areas, including the new budgetary surveillance mechanisms. Technically, a country which persists in running an excessive deficit is liable to be fined by the finance ministers. But in practice such fines are unlikely to be imposed. It is much more likely that peer-group pressure—perhaps going as far as public reprimands—would force the miscreant into line.

Similarly, the EU's recent agreements on company taxation have involved guidelines rather than hard rules. On CO_2 emissions, governments will decide themselves how to meet the standards agreed on in Kyoto. This approach would also suit several aspects of police and customs co-operation. Arguably it could apply to those parts of social policy which do not have to be harmonised for the sake of the single market, and to local environmental standards such as clean beaches. In all these areas the Commission can monitor progress and report to the Council of Ministers and to the Parliament on which countries are failing to meet the standards.

Of course this new approach could not apply to policy areas which require detailed central rules, such as those concerning the single market. There is not much point in having a broad agreement to curb coal subsidies unless the competition directorate can encourage the Germans to comply by threatening a prosecution.

It is quite possible that a voluntary approach may prove inadequate in some areas; perhaps member-states will fail to constrain their budget deficits or meet the Kyoto targets. Jean Monnet would surely disapprove of this devolved style of policy-making: he believed in a stark dichotomy between inter-governmental decision-making, which required unanimity and was thus inefficient, and supranational decision-making, which involved majority voting and was thus effective. But it would be ridiculous for the EU to legislate in detail in every area that it touched. The new approach should be given a chance. If it later transpires that it does not work in some or other area, the Monnet method can be applied.

Another way of making the Union less strange and remote is to make it more transparent. The Amsterdam treaty provides for public access to most EU documents—though unfortunately it allows the Council of Ministers to define the rules for access—and for records of how ministers voted to be revealed. These are only very small steps in the right direction. The Council of Ministers remains the only law-making body in the world which normally meets in secret. When it meets as a legislature (as opposed to an executive) it should be televised.

That reform would not in itself make the Union more popular; few people would want to watch such tedious proceedings for long. But the occasional highlight on the television news of some important debate, for example the pros and cons of legislation for an EU-wide energy tax, would help, in a modest way, to demystify the Union. A minister who defended the interests of the chemicals industry in opposing such a tax, in front of millions of viewers in his and other countries, might find a large postbag.

Officials complain that the arrival of television cameras in the Council of Ministers would achieve little, since deal-making would migrate to the corridors. But that is not the point. Ministers might deal in the corridors, but on camera they would still have to justify the line they were taking to the people who elected them. The more that people see the insides of the Union, however dull they may be, the less likely they are to be scared of it.

The EU institutions should place as much of their documentation as possible—including working papers and draft laws—on the internet, and invite public responses. The main beneficiaries would be the media, NGOs and interested pressure groups, but the greater openness might eventually do something for the EU's image in the eyes of ordinary citizens.

Monetary union also needs to be made more transparent. The Maastricht model of a European Central Bank that is independent of any political pressure is now immutable. The Germans extracted that model as the price for sacrificing the D-mark. The "New Zealand model", which blends both democratic control and operational independence, would have been preferable. The New Zealand parliament instructs the central bank governor to deliver a given level of inflation. The central bank has complete independence over the monetary policy it chooses in pursuit of that goal. When the governor reports back to the parliament he may be sacked if he has failed in his task.

The European Union, however, is unlikely to amend the Maastricht treaty's provisions on EMU for many decades. Until such time as that is possible the EU needs to moderate the ECB's brazen unaccountability in ways that do not breach the treaty. Wim Duisenberg, the ECB president, has agreed to report regularly to the European Parliament. But he has also said that he will not go to national parliaments and that he does not want to release minutes of ECB board meetings for 15 years.

Alan Donnelly, the leader of the Labour MEPs in Strasbourg, has put forward a scheme under which Mr Duisenberg and the other ECB board members would report regularly to a forum consisting of MEPs and members of national parliaments' finance committees. And Mr Donnelly has argued that the minutes of board meetings should be released within a month.

These ideas are sensible. So long as the ECB's directors make an effort to explain their monetary policy, and the reasons for it, the bank's independence may not vex the public too much. They should become expert at written and spoken communication, appearing often on television and writing frequently for newspapers. For there will be times when the ECB has to take unpopular decisions. If it is seen as a distant, arrogant and secretive organisation, it may turn European public opinion off EMU in particular and the European Union in general.

In defence of Strasbourg

The lack of a strong feeling of Europeanness among EU citizens probably limits the amount of democracy that can be achieved at Union level. European elections are fought principally on domestic political issues. And those elections do not change the EU's government: there is no executive responsible to the European Parliament. Executive authority rests in the Council of Ministers and in the European Commission, which both contain figures from all the main political families. As yet, pan-European federations of political parties have little clout.

The traditional, federalist response to the democratic deficit has been to boost the powers of the Commission and the Parliament so that, eventually, the political structures of the EU resemble those of a nation state: the Commission would be an executive responsible to the Parliament, while the Council would become a kind of upper house. But it is not self-evident that this approach would plug the deficit. For if the institutions developed along the lines of the federalist model, the Union would inevitably become stronger. And that could easily worsen the problem that such reforms were supposed to tackle, namely that many people do not want the EU's distant institutions to be so powerful.

Thus making the institutions more accountable may not necessarily make them more legitimate. Given that the European demos is, at best, underdeveloped, and given that the main focus of political identification in Europe is still the nation-state, the Union should not attempt to replicate the political structures of the nation-state at the European level.

The European Parliament is certainly an unfashionable institution, and not only in Britain. In the summer of 1998, when Tony Blair and Robin Cook engaged in brainstorming sessions with their officials, some of them suggested scrapping a directly-elected parliament altogether. The Foreign Office came up with a plan for a committee of national parliamentarians that would vet EU laws on grounds of subsidiarity and proportionality, and which might in time evolve into an upper house of the European Parliament. It also proposed giving the European Council (that is, summits of heads of government) an enhanced role in setting the EU's strategic priorities. It would meet every three months, instead of every six, and give both the Council of Ministers and the Commission a three-year rolling work programme.

The basic sentiment behind these ideas, that the EU's legitimacy could be improved if national institutions played a greater role in its workings, is ˙sensible. It is undeniable that the European Parliament has not yet learned to use its considerable powers in ways that appear interesting, important or relevant to many EU citizens.

However, EU institutions cannot depend entirely upon indirect democracy for their accountability and legitimacy. It is not sufficient that the Council of Ministers consists of elected politicians, and that the president of the Commission is appointed by elected prime ministers. If the institutions are to carry out an increasingly complex array of tasks effectively, they will need to derive legitimacy not only from national governments but also from direct elections. The Union should not imitate the constitutional structures of the nation-state but, as a unique political system, it needs bespoke structures of its own. It will be argued below that the Union needs not only an elected Parliament but also elected commissioners.

The government is right to argue that national parliaments should take a closer interest in EU legislation. The Amsterdam treaty says that the Council of Ministers should not consider a Commission proposal for six weeks after it is made available, so that governments have time to pass it to their national parliaments. The treaty gives "COSAC", a committee that brings together the heads of European affairs committees of national parliaments and a delegation of MEPs, a formal right to express opinions on EU legislation.

In Britain, the two House of Commons scrutiny committees for EU legislation suffer from insufficient expertise, resources and channels of communication with EU institutions—though the House of Lords committee has a better record. The Commons committees often lack the time to give important Commission proposals due attention.

There should be more contact between Westminster and the European Parliament. British MPs are allowed only one paid trip a year to EU institutions—and few avail themselves of that right. MEPs are treated like aliens in the Commons or Lords. National and European parliamentarians should be able to attend each others' committees. In particular, *rapporteurs*—members of European Parliament committees who write reports on draft laws—should be encouraged to present their reports to committees of national parliaments.

The Foreign Office idea for a pan-European committee of national parliamentarians to scrutinise EU laws, building on COSAC, is promising. But the British should not propose that it evolve into an upper house to the Strasbourg assembly. The Union has too many institutions as it is, and the creation of another would make the legislative process—which already involves the Commission, the Council of Ministers, the Economic and Capital Social Committee, the Committee of the Regions and the Parliament—even slower. Such a proposal would be seen as a direct attack on the European Parliament and might lose Britain some potential allies.

National MPs should certainly consider European directives, and pass on their views to the relevant representative in the Council of Ministers, but there is a limit to the role that they can usefully play in EU affairs. National MPs, quite properly, tend to focus on what is going on in their own country. Few of them have the time, inclination or expertise to follow European legislation closely. So they are therefore ill-suited to call either the Commission or the Council of Ministers to account, in the same way that county councillors are the wrong people to check the executive in London.

One former MEP who later went to the Commons and served on an EU scrutiny committee dismisses the idea that MPs can usefully monitor EU legislation. "Those who turn up to the Commons scrutiny committees have seldom read the paperwork and they generally only ask about their own hobbyhorses," says the MP. "But because Strasbourg is principally a committee-based Parliament, a lot of the MEPs there build up real expertise. They can focus on the details of legislation in ways that MPs cannot."

Would it not help if the Commons' various departmental select committees established sub-committees to scrutinise relevant EU laws, as already happens in the Lords? The MP is sceptical. "Westminster MPs have so many other things to focus on, such as constituency work and media demands, that they would find it hard to develop the expertise that would be required for such subcommittees. I can't see many of the brighter MPs thinking that it would do their careers any good to serve on specialist sub-committees."

In any case, given that the Council of Ministers passes much EU legislation by majority vote, there is a limit to the influence that Westminster MPs can wield. Even if they persuade a minister to support a particular position, he or she may be outvoted in Brussels. But when the law reaches the European Parliament, British MEPs may be able to amend it; hence the importance of links between the two sorts of parliamentarian.

To misquote Churchill, the European Parliament is the worst means yet invented for injecting some democracy into the EU, except for all the others that have been tried from time to time. The Parliament's legislative track record is in fact more impressive than many of its critics would imagine. It has generally used its power of co-decision—which gives it an equal say with the Council of Ministers on many sorts of law—responsibly.

Parliament's amendments to directives are often an improvement and sometimes suggest that it is more in tune with public opinion than the Council of Ministers. Take the recent directive harmonising biotechnology patent law. The initial text from the Council and the Commission addressed the concern of biotech companies that patent law be brought into line with American and Japanese practice. But the text ignored strongly-felt public concerns on animal welfare and medical ethics, so Parliament rejected it. Only in May 1998, when ministers had accepted about 70 parliamentary amendments—so that, for example, the directive bans human cloning and the modification of human genes in ways that could be inherited—did Parliament pass it. The outcome is a reasonable compromise between the needs of the industry and public concerns.

Most Britons would be surprised to know how eagerly the Parliament's pronouncements on foreign policy are listened to in many parts of the world. For it is capable of using its power over budget lines and its right to reject international treaties to some effect. Thus the Parliament's

criticism of Vladimir Meciar's illiberal government has heartened the
Slovak opposition; the Slovak government knows that the Parliament
can exclude it from the "Phare" aid programme. In 1995 the Parliament
held up approval of the EU's customs union with Turkey, until the latter
agreed to remove some anti-Kurdish clauses from its constitution.

Members of the Commission and the Council have to appear before the
Parliament to answer questions and explain their views. In 1997 a
parliamentary committee of inquiry into BSE recommended that the
Commission's responsibility for food safety be taken out of the agriculture
directorate. Like all agriculture ministries it had grown too close to
farming interests. The Commission followed that advice and gave Emma
Bonino, the consumer affairs commissioner, responsibility for food safety.

The European Parliament's budgetary control committee already plays a
useful role in scrutinising EU spending. For example, in 1997 it revealed
that Commission officials had covered up fraud—involving phoney
contracts—in the tourism directorate; as a result Commission officials
were sacked. The committee could do a lot more to ensure that EU funds
are spent efficiently. In fact several continental governments are
sympathetic to the view sometimes heard in London that this committee
could evolve into a more powerful body, along the lines of the Commons'
Public Accounts Committee.

The budgetary control committee did most of the work for the Parliament's
committee of inquiry—chaired by Labour MEP John Tomlinson—into
"transit fraud". The committee's report, which appeared in 1997,
examined the problem of goods and farm produce that are supposedly
bound for non-EU countries and thus exempted from tax while travelling
within the Union. It is common for the accompanying documentation to
be forged, and for the goods to be diverted for sale inside the EU. Thus a
fifth of all cigarettes sold in Spain are thought to be contraband. The
report estimated that transit fraud costs 15-20 billion ecus a year, of which
three quarters is a cost to national exchequers, and a quarter to the EU
budget. This report has led to steps being taken to create a pan-European
computer network to monitor goods in transit.

Despite such excellent work—largely unnoticed by the European media
—the budgetary control committee lacks the resources to focus on many

complex areas of the EU budget. It needs a larger secretariat and the capacity to call on expert help. It should be allowed to question national officials: it is often forgotten that national administrations spend 80 per cent of the EU's budget (principally the CAP and the structural funds). And it should consider establishing specialist sub-committees for each of the main areas of EU spending.

The budgetary control committee has few links with the Court of Auditors, the EU's spending watchdog. If the two bodies could develop organic links they would both benefit: one has political nous, the other technical expertise. For example the committee could point the Court in certain directions, as the Commons Public Accounts Committee does with the National Audit Office, while leaving it operationally independent.

The better MEPs have the knowledge, understanding and access to information which makes them the right people to hold the Commission to account and to amend EU legislation. National parliamentarians do not. For all these reasons the Labour government should not ignore the role that European Parliament can play in ameliorating the democratic deficit. But the Parliament should not be the only directly-elected European institution.

Democratising the commission

It is hard to defend the existing method of choosing the president of the European Comission. The president plays a crucial role, personifying the Union and its aspirations. The job involves steering the Commission's work programme, acting as an honest broker among the EU heads of government and representing the Union—alongside the prime minister of the country holding the presidency—to the rest of the world.

Yet the president is chosen, at present, in an unseemly horse-trade among heads of government. Thus in 1994 Helmut Kohl vetoed the Netherlands' Ruud Lubbers because he had taken a personal dislike to him; John Major then vetoed Belgium's Jean-Luc Dehaene, the Franco-German choice, on the grounds that he was too federalist; and in the end everyone agreed on Luxembourg's Jacques Santer, equally federalist but innocuous.

Early in 1998 Jacques Delors—who as a president had been federalist but far from innocuous—put forward a scheme for choosing the president by a new method. He suggested that the main pan-European federations of political parties should each campaign in the next European elections with a president-designate at their head. The Party of European Socialists might choose, say, Felipe González; the European Peoples Party (christian democrats and conservatives), Wolfgang Schäuble; and the liberals, Sir Peter Sutherland. The heads of government would agree, in advance, to select the candidate of the party which won the most seats in the elections.

This plan would certainly stir up some interest in the European elections. It would encourage the existing pan-European parties to become more solid entities. Its ingenuity is to change the method of selecting the president without amending the treaties: legally, the European Council would still appoint the president, subject to a vote of confidence from the European Parliament.

The snags with the Delors plan are that cross-border party structures may be too weak to ensure that every national component of a party federation supports the same candidate; that there may be too few potential candidates well enough known to have popular appeal in more than a handful of countries; and that the heads of government would be unlikely give up their prerogative to choose the president.

A second scheme for choosing the president was proposed in one of the first CER pamphlets.[13] The European Council would choose a shortlist of suitable candidates. Each of them would then face hearings from a committee of the European Parliament, live on television. Depending on how the candidates performed, and on their views, the full Parliament would then vote on who should become Commission president. This scheme, like Mr Delors', could be implemented without changing the treaties. But the heads of government would have to promise to endorse whichever candidate won the parliamentary vote. And they might object to this scheme, like Mr Delors', on the grounds that it would increase the legitimacy and authority of the Commission president.

[13] See essay by Charles Grant in "Visions for the future", CER, 1996

A group of Foreign Office diplomats has floated a surprisingly radical plan for electing the entire commission. Rival multinational slates of would-be commissioners would contest pan-European elections at the same time as the elections for the European Parliament. In practice the contest would probably be between the centre-left and the centre-right. The argument is that such elections would give people the sense that they had some control over the EU, and that it was not run just by faceless bureaucrats.

These diplomats think that an accountable Commission would be obliged to improve the quality of its policies and management, that it would be less susceptible to pressure from interest groups and that it would also be more likely to pursue popular policies. And since the commissioners would be united around a common programme, the institution would be more internally coherent than it is today.

Such a plan would encourage the development of European political parties and would, the diplomats believe, help to start creating a European demos. But they would balance this boost to the Commission's authority by defining its powers more narrowly than do the current treaties.

One problem with this scheme is that it could harm rather than—as the diplomats intend—help the Commission's legitimacy. Suppose that a right-wing slate, swept to power in the Commission elections, started to promote policies that were opposed by a left-wing government in Britain and by a majority of the British people: the EU's legitimacy in Britain would be undermined. The EU has always worked by drawing together people from different countries and political persuasions and getting them to agree, through delicate and often painstaking processes, on common positions. Turning EU politics into a fight between left and right, or any other set of opposites, could damage rather than repair popular perceptions of Brussels. The other obvious objection to this scheme, like most of the others described here, is that governments would not agree to anything which risked increasing the Commission's ability to stand up to them.

A proposal: national elections for European commissioners

Having considered various schemes for making the Commission more democratic, this author would suggest a system of national elections for European commissioners. The proposal is based on the following assumptions: that the European Commission should retain its principal functions; that an enlarged Union of some 25 countries with, inevitably, a degree of variable geometry, will probably require a stronger Commission to ensure that everyone respects the single market and that the institutional complexities do not prevent effective decision-making; and that the greatest threat to the Union's future development, including its enlargement, is public hostility to EU institutions, notably because of their lack of legitimacy.

The proposal also assumes that within a few years there is likely to be only one commissioner per country; that a pan-European system of election is for the time being not feasible, given the under-developed state of the European demos and the federations of political parties; and that EU institutions are more likely to gain legitimacy from a direct connection to national political systems than from pan-European elections.

The proposal is that each country should hold its own direct election for a European commissioner. In Britain each party would put up a candidate, so that the contest would be held between, say, Neil Kinnock, Sir Leon Brittan and Lord Steel, on the same day as the European parliamentary elections. The European Council would then choose one of the new commissioners as president. The president would allot portfolios among his or her commissioners. The commissioners' terms would be non-renewable. The European Parliament would have the right to sack individual commissioners that it considered corrupt or grossly incompetent, on a two thirds vote.

Thus the Commission would derive its legitimacy from national electorates and from the European Council. It would be responsible to the European Parliament. This new method of choosing the Commission would create considerable interest in European elections and institutions. It should ensure a higher quality of commissioner, especially from countries such as Germany which in the past have tended to send second-raters to Brussels.

Federalists do not like this scheme. They fear that its emphasis on national rather than pan-European voting would hinder the development of a European political community. They may or may not be right that contests between slates of notables from several countries would nurture the embryonic demos. But there is even less chance of governments agreeing to pan-European than national elections of commissioners.

A second criticism of the proposal is that elected commissioners would find it harder to fulfil the Commission's core responsibility of representing the European interest, as opposed to their own national interest. In order to win election, candidates might promise to help any number of special interests. And once the commissioner was installed in Brussels he or she might shamelessly promote his country's or party's priorities.

That would be a danger if the commissioners were able to seek re-election. But there is no particular reason why commissioners elected for a single term should be more nationalistic than those currently appointed by governments, who are eligible for second terms. The reality today is that all commissioners represent national interests to a greater or lesser degree. Thus when the Commission adopted Sir Leon Brittan's scheme for a New Transatlantic Marketplace, in the spring of 1998, the French commissioners followed their government line by opposing the proposals. It is sometimes desirable that the Commission does take into account national viewpoints, so that it does not propose too many laws of the abolish-the-British-pint variety that hurt national sensibilities.

In essence, however, the Commission should remain the body that seeks to promote the general interest against the particular interests of states. So when the elected commissioners arrive in Brussels, they should—like members of the board of the European Central Bank—act with independence.

A third criticism—and one heard within the Foreign Office—is that having non-renewable terms of office would invalidate the whole idea of making the Commission more accountable. If commissioners could not seek re-election, electorates would not be able to "kick the rascals out". That is true, but the commissioners would be responsible to and sackable by the European Parliament. And so long as national electorates could "kick the rascals in", if only once, in a contested election, the Commission's democratic credentials would be greatly strengthened.

The fourth criticism is that the Commission should be placing a greater emphasis on managing and policing the market, rather than writing new laws. Elections for commissioners would make the institution more political, when it should be becoming more technocratic.

The fifth criticism is that governments would never agree to a reform that would increase the Commission's power. No prime minister will be in a hurry to approve a scheme that would create a rival focus of authority within his own country, and one that could be from a different party. Who knows, prime minister Blair might have to contend with commissioner Portillo.

The answers to these two criticisms are related. Governments will always find that, in the short run, the arguments for keeping the Commission unelected are overwhelming. For years they have wanted to have their cake and eat it, keeping the Commission an illegitimate and unpopular institution but expecting it to perform a wide array of complex and difficult tasks. And this has just about worked.

But they will not be able to have their cake and eat it for ever. There is not much chance of governments agreeing to elected commissioners within, say, the next five years, but they may rethink when they reflect on how the EU is likely to develop over the coming decades. As the Union expands eastwards, the Commission will be responsible for reforming the internal policies and for handling the accession negotiations. The tasks of managing the variable geometry and the market will be more complex and harder than they are today. A Commission that is denied legitimacy will lack the strength required to carry out these roles effectively.

The Union is unlikely to reach a settled, final steady state. It will remain in flux, responding to as yet unforeseen challenges. Thus the Commission will have to remain both a technocratic and a political body. In any case, it is hard to distinguish between the executive and political roles that the Commission would need in order to push through say, another round of CAP reform. One of the Commission's most crucial roles will be to provide the Union with some political leadership.

The Labour government should be in favour of a Union whose institutions have the authority to ensure that the rules are respected. It should therefore think seriously about giving the Commission some democratic credentials, so that it becomes more acceptable to ordinary people. Of course there is a risk that the British commissioner might come from a different party to the government. But that is the case with the current system of appointed commissioners: when Mr Blair took office Britain's senior commissioner was the Conservative Sir Leon Brittan. As for the danger that elections for commissioners might install Michael Portillo in Brussels, an appointment—by prime minister William Hague or John Redwood—could produce the same result. In any event, elected commissioners, whether Eurosceptic or a Europhile, would have a strong incentive to behave responsibly; those that charged around like a bull in a china shop would soon gain a reputation for incompetence back home.

If the Commission remains as illegitimate as it is today, the happiest people will be Eurosceptics. For they know that the weakest link in the armour of pro-Europeans is the undemocratic and ineffective nature of EU institutions. As Mark Leonard has argued, there is a close correlation between the legitimacy of institutions and their effectiveness. A Commission that does not believe in its own legitimacy will be less willing to stand up to member-states and is more likely to ally itself to particular lobbies or interests.

Governments might be more willing to accept elections for commissioners if at the same time they could find ways of clipping the Commission's wings. They could define the areas in which it can propose binding legislation more narrowly than do the current treaties. Since the Commission has tended to make a poor job of managing EU programmes, such as aid to Eastern Europe and to the developing countries, some of its administrative tasks could be hived off to independent agencies. And the Parliament could (as mentioned above) be given a greater role in scrutinising the efficiency with which the Commission spends money.

All about results

Various sorts of institutional reform can certainly help to make the Union more acceptable to its people. But in the long run the Union will flourish or perish according to the success, or otherwise, of its ventures, and the ability, or otherwise, of political leaders to communicate such achievements as there are.

The EU has to cope with at least four major challenges in order to win the respect of its citizens. First, it should ensure that enlargement into Eastern Europe, and the related budgetary, agricultural and regional policy reforms, proceed smoothly.

Second, EU governments will have to make a better job of co-ordinating foreign policy. If they can do no better than wring their hands over Kosovo, if they fail to untangle their knotted relations with Cyprus and Turkey, and if they appear unable to act without American leadership, the Union's credibility will suffer a grievous blow on both sides of the Atlantic.

Third, EU unemployment has to fall far below its current average level of 10.5 per cent. Although the Union's policies cannot in themselves make much impact, if continental governments could find the right measures to shorten the dole queues it would do wonders for the EU's image.

The fourth and related challenge, and probably the most important of all, is to make a success of monetary union. If EMU engenders rows, recession, crises and instability, not only the euro but also the whole Union may be damaged beyond the point of repair. But if—as appears more likely—the ECB and the finance ministers can deliver low inflation, low interest rates and economic growth, and if the euro-zone appears as a haven of stability in a world of financial turmoil, public opinion will swiftly latch on to the practical benefits and back the project.

However, even a long list of EU achievements will not do much for its reputation unless politicians make an effort to explain and to praise them. It is worth remembering that British opinion moved sharply pro-EU in the late 1980s, when Lord Young of Graffham and other ministers sang the praises of the thoroughly successful single-market project. Shifting public opinion from its current hostility should not prove an impossible task. Numerous surveys of attitudes to the EU suggests that many peoples' views are ambiguous—they both like and dislike aspects of European integration—and shallowly held.

The politicians' task would be easier if people understood the EU better. A Eurobarometer survey in 1996 found that 89 per cent of Britons wanted schools to teach how EU institutions worked. But the schools do not: the EU does not even feature in the core curriculum of A level politics. The government should ensure that an understanding of both the EU and NATO—the two central planks of British foreign policy—is part of the basic core curriculum.

For the last ten years that the Conservatives held power, ministers almost never had a good word to say about the Union. The fact that the Labour government has already abandoned anti-EU rhetoric seems to have affected public opinion. A wide range of polling data suggests that hostility to the EU has fallen since the last election.

Business leaders, too, need to be readier to stick their heads above the parapet and explain why the EU is good for jobs. They have been reluctant to do so without political cover. Both they and politicians should be readier to speak out boldly, to face down Europhobic newspaper editors and to support each other.

6 Europe's shifting balance of power

The strains in the Franco-German relationship

Despite Labour's decision to stay out of the euro until at least 2002, the task of rebuilding British influence is not an impossible one. In some ways the current situation suits Britain very well. Mr Blair's government has, in its first 18 months, done much to restore good relations with its EU partners. His popularity at home, his positive attitude to the EU, his influence in Washington and the strength of the British economy ensure that other EU leaders listen to him with respect.

Meanwhile the Franco-German alliance, the dominant force in EU politics for the past 35 years, is probably in a shakier state than at any time since de Gaulle and Adenauer stitched it together. One symptom of this shakiness, and of the possibilities of a realignment in European power politics, was the decision in July 1998 of the London and Frankfurt stock exchanges to merge. Neither consulted the Paris Bourse, although it had been negotiating a merger with the Frankfurt exchange. The French establishment was shocked, and even more so when Rolf Breuer, the chairman of Deutsche Bank, talked of the Bourse being admitted as a junior partner, with a 20 per cent shareholding, in the new venture. The Frankfurt stock exchange, of course, is independent of the German government. But a few years ago it would have been inconceivable for the Germans to keep the French in the dark over such a move.

The personalities of the French and German leaders are part of the problem, for the Franco-German alliance has always been driven from the top downwards. Helmut Kohl and François Mitterrand enjoyed a close friendship. Mr Kohl and Mr Chirac do not get on. Mr Kohl is in any case probably near the end of his distinguished career. President Chirac has still not recovered from losing the May 1997 general election. Both men appear tired and uninspiring. France's prime minister, Lionel Jospin, has more wind in his sails, but the combination of a Gaullist president and a Socialist prime minister somewhat constrains France's diplomatic power.

The Chancellery in Bonn finds Mr Chirac untrustworthy. The Germans have still not forgiven him for announcing a series of major defence reforms in 1996—abandoning conscription, creating a rapid-reaction capability and scrapping some Franco-German armaments projects—without consulting them. Subsequent French foot-dragging on the conversion of Airbus into a single corporate entity and on the cross-border restructuring of the European defence industry has annoyed Bonn.

So did Mr Chirac's stubborn insistence at the May 1998 EU summit that Jean-Claude Trichet should replace Wim Duisenberg as ECB president after four years, when all the other governments had agreed to back Mr Duisenberg for a full eight-year term. The fact that French trade unions have proven so effective at derailing government attempts to reform the labour market is one reason why German policy makers worry about the ability of the French economy to modernise. A worried Joachim Bitterlich, Mr Kohl's chief foreign policy adviser and a noted Francophile, asked friends in Washington in early 1998, "does France have a future?".

Meanwhile Gerhard Schröder, the SPD's chancellor candidate, displays some of the traditional anglophilia of a North German. He looks to New Labour and to Tony Blair as his model. Having talked of the need for a triple alliance between Britain, France and Germany in the spring of 1998, he has subsequently sounded more cautious on this sensitive subject. But he has little knowledge of France and there is no doubt that he is less fixed on a special relationship between France and Germany than Mr Kohl.

In July 1998 Mr Schröder said that he would voice Germany's interests as forcefully as France voiced its interests. "I really want these ties to be more strongly determined by visions of the future than by the burden of the past," he said. "Franco-German relations under a new government will be just as important as they have been in the past. But here, it will also apply that it is a relationship of two self-confident partners." Translation: we are not going to let the French push us around so much as we did.[14]

[14] International Herald Tribune, 27.7.98

Many other countries in the EU, long resentful of Franco-German dominance, would be delighted if Britain could become more positive and assertive, and less defensive and reactive in EU councils. However, the British always over-estimate the strains in the Franco-German axis. And they usually under-estimate its underlying strengths.

That alliance remains a vital force on the European diplomatic scene. Thus in May 1998, while Mr Blair was preparing to make institutional reform an important part of the agenda for the June summit, Mr Kohl and Mr Chirac to some extent upstaged him with a joint letter on reforming the Union. They had not consulted Mr Blair about their letter. Indeed, France and Germany never do consult Britain over their joint initiatives.

To understand the glue that holds France and Germany together it is worth considering the origins of this special relationship. Thrice invaded in a hundred years, France's rationale for the alliance is based on its fear of Germany. Given Germany's preponderant economic strength in the EU, France hopes that its close alliance with Germany will allow it some measure of control, or at least influence, over what Germany does with its weight. For 30 years France has had more say than any other country over the development of the EU, largely because it has garnered German support for its initiatives.

After the war Germany was a pariah state that craved respectability and normality. EU membership in general, and the Franco-German alliance in particular offered Germany a way back into the routine world of international negotiations. Working with France, usually in a junior role, Germany was able to achieve considerable influence. If Germany had thrown its weight around on its own, or in alliance with a smaller and clearly subordinate country, it would have risked inciting old fears of German dominance and arrogance. The great worry of Germany's post-war strategists has been that their country would become surrounded by an alliance of hostile of countries. Helmut Kohl, his perspective strongly influenced by the war, has always seen the alliance with France as a defining characteristic of modern Germany.

Whatever the current strains, the top politicians and officials in each country consider a special alliance with the other to be fundamentally in the national self-interest. The Elysée Treaty, signed by General de Gaulle and Konrad Adenauer in 1963, institutionalised a wide range of links—cultural, administrative and political—between the two countries. Since then the French president and the German chancellor have met at least twice a year, the foreign and defence ministers at least four times a year and senior officials at least once a month. The treaty says that "the two governments will consult before any decision on all important questions of foreign policy, with a view to reaching as far as possible an analogous position". All the exchanges and meetings have helped the French and German elites to understand each other intimately. Thus Britain could not instantly create such a close relationship with either France or Germany, however hard it tried.

Indeed, one reason why the Franco-German alliance has proven so resilient is that each knows that the other will accept certain ground rules. For example, however much the pair argue, they will virtually always, at the end of the day, agree on a compromise. And each will, if necessary, sacrifice important interests for the sake of an agreement in which the other gives up some of its interests. For example in the spring of 1988, when Mitterrand persuaded Mr Kohl to accept that Jacques Delors should chair a committee of central bank governors on EMU, Mr Kohl's price was that France should agree to the liberalisation of capital movements within the EU. Again, at Maastricht in 1991, the French ceded more power than they would have wished to the European Parliament, because that was a Kohl priority; in return the Germans gave in to various French wishes, including the setting of 1999 as the starting date for EMU. Such bargains are the lifeblood of the Franco-German relationship.

The second main reason why the relationship has proven so resilient is that neither France nor Germany trusts Britain. For all their differences, France and Germany agree that the EU has a purpose, albeit a vaguely defined one: ever closer union. The French and the Germans quite rightly suspect that many Britons do not share that goal. They often fear that Britain's European agenda is to create a free-trade area with a few bits and pieces added on.

While not all Britons share that Thatcherite perspective, it is undoubtedly true that Britain has either shunned or tried to sabotage many of the key steps in European integration: in 1960 it created the European Free Trade Association in a bid to undermine the nascent European Economic Community; having finally joined the EEC in 1973, it insisted in 1975 on renegotiating its terms of entry; it shunned the Exchange Rate Mechanism in 1979—only to leave two years after Mrs Thatcher finally took Britain into the ERM in 1990; during the long negotiations which culminated in the Maastricht treaty's, Britain used its many diplomatic skills in repeated efforts to block moves towards monetary union; and it would not accept the treaty's Social Chapter, agreed in 1991, until 1997.

Few Britons appreciate the extent to which—despite the arrival of a more EU-friendly government—Britain is still mistrusted on the continent. Britain will have to behave in a constructive manner for several years, before it can win the trust of its partners.

Nevertheless the fact that the Franco-German relationship is structurally weaker than it has been for many years does offer Britain opportunities. German reunification has changed the balance of power within that relationship by strengthening Germany. The French also worry about the effect of the forthcoming expansion of the EU: Germany rather than France will be at the heart of the new Europe, surrounded by countries that could become its potential economic and political satellites. Thus France is more concerned than ever to contain Germany through a close alliance.

However, the German need for the Franco-German alliance is diminishing with time. The younger generation of German politicians, such as the Wolfgang Schäuble and Volker Rühe of the christian democrats, or Mr Schröder, are not so marked by the war as Mr Kohl. They are less reluctant than he has been to assert Germany's interests in a direct manner. They do not feel such a strong need for the respectability that the French alliance bestows upon Germany.

Can Britain learn to make friends?

Whether the Franco-German alliance continues to lead the EU, though with much less strength and clarity of purpose than in the past, or whether it is replaced by a more open system of alliances, with Britain playing an important role, depends on how the British play their cards. The first thing the British have to do is learn to make friends on the continent. They have managed brief liaisons on particular subjects, such as budget reform, but have not been good at longer-term relationships. The politics of the EU is a subtle and complex game in which country A may do country B a favour, in return for it supporting A's most cherished policies. But Britain, more than most member-states, has a tendency to treat each issue in isolation, thereby missing the chance to make trade-offs and win friends. Too often Britain has been reluctant to listen to its partners and unwilling to engage them in the joint analysis of problems.

Britain's policy on Europe has generally followed Palmerston's comment to the House of Commons in 1848 that "we have no eternal allies and we have no perpetual enemies. Our interests are eternal and perpetual, and those interests it is our duty to follow". Britain's only significant strategic alliance is with the United States, particularly on military matters and intelligence: governments of right and left have supported US military actions, and the British have been repaid with favours, for example during the Falklands War.

Is there scope for Britain to form long-term alliances in Europe? For the time being it is probably not feasible for Britain to seek strategic alliances, in the sense of making a long-term commitment to a country, through thick and thin. In the longer run such alliances might be possible, when Britain has clarified its vision of the kind of Europe it wants. What Mr Blair can do right away—without trying to supplant either the French or the Germans in each others' affections—is make a big effort to improve bilateral relations with France, Germany and the other EU states. Encouragingly, there are signs that he is trying to do this.

Of the larger EU countries, Germany appears to offer the best prospects. Britain and Germany disagree on whether much more European integration is a good idea. But they agree on many other subjects. As the two largest net contributors to the EU budget, Britain and Germany believe in imposing financial discipline on the Union. Both are instinctive free traders: in May 1998, when France vetoed the Commission's plans for a "New Transatlantic Marketplace", intended to create a single market between the EU and the United States, it angered the German government as much as the British. And both believe in the creation of a pan-European defence industry, firmly bedded in the private sector. Britain and Germany think it important to maintain America's commitment to European defence and worry that French prickliness may undermine it.

They are the strongest supporters of enlarging the EU into Eastern Europe. And if Mr Schröder wins the September 1998 elections, Germany will be led by an overt Anglophile.

Ties with France may prove harder to nurture. France's economy becomes a little more liberal every year, but its politicians are still more inherently protectionist than most others in the EU. Its views on CAP reform (like those of Bavaria) will often be diametrically opposed to those of Britain. Furthermore, many Frenchmen still share de Gaulle's view that Britain is a Trojan horse for the United States in Europe. And they are certainly right that in a military crisis Britain's first instinct is normally to turn to the United States.

The fact that both Blair and Jospin are Socialists may not mean much. Each of them knows that, on economic policy, Blair is more of a free marketeer than many right-of-centre politicians on the continent. Contacts between the Labour Party and the Parti Socialiste have never been strong. But by the summer of 1998 it was evident that, after an initially cool relationship, Mr Blair and Mr Jospin were starting to get on well. Mr Blair understands that in French terms Mr Jospin is a moderniser, and he appreciates that the French prime minister is having to modernise under much greater constraints—such as Communist ministers and vociferous trade unions—than he did.

While the Foreign Office tends to promote the value of an alliance with Germany, 10 Downing Street emphasises that France and Britain have a common philosophical approach to the Union. The French and British governments want it to remain in essence a union of states. And both want to give the Union more legitimacy by boosting the role of national or nationally-based institutions (the European Council, the Council of Ministers and national parliaments). Even on economics, Mr Jospin is the most liberal and pragmatic leader France has had for many years. He has privatised more companies than the previous right-wing government and—unusually for a Frenchman—celebrated America's economic success. Meanwhile some of those close to Mr Blair regard Mr Schröder as an unknown and therefore slightly dangerous quantity.

But the British will have to work hard to woo the hearts of the French. As a senior French diplomat put it: "When Blair went to Paris, he spoke to the National Assembly; when Clinton came to London he addressed Parliament; but when Jospin came to London [in July 1998] he addressed the Foreign Policy Centre [a pro-Labour think-tank]. We feel you are not that interested in getting close to us."

There is certainly scope for an Anglo-French alliance on foreign policy and defence. The two post-imperial nations may differ on how to react to crises such as that in February 1998 over weapons inspections in Iraq. But they are the only EU members that often have a global perspective and a sense of responsibility for international peace and stability. Both have talented diplomatic corps and the ability to project military power. Their close collaboration over Bosnia—both in the diplomacy of trying to end the war and in the provision of peacekeeping troops—has shown that the two countries can work well together. They should be in the forefront of trying to make the EU's foreign policy machinery more effective, and in developing the European defence identity.

Mr Blair should suggest to the French and German governments that Britain shadow some provisions of the Elysée treaty with each of them. There would be no need for formalities or fanfares. Mr Blair could simply ask his senior ministers to meet their opposite numbers in France and Germany, say twice a year, and to stay in touch on the telephone. Similarly, senior officials could meet their equivalents on a regular basis. An effort should be made find policy areas that are ripe for common analyses. With France, for example, Britain could try to work on a joint approach to Russia's problems, and with Germany it could develop a common line on reforming EU competition policy.

The creation of "virtual" Elysée treaties with France and Germany would lead to a lot of extra meetings. That might appear to be an uninspiring way of augmenting British influence. But over a period of time all the meetings should—as the Franco-German relationship has shown—help to create a climate of trust, understanding and consultation that could only be beneficial.

On one matter or another, Britain should be able to forge alliances with virtually all the EU countries. Spain, Italy and the Netherlands share a strong interest with Britain in ensuring that France and Germany do not dominate everything. Mr Blair's recent decision to establish annual

summits with the Italian and Spanish prime ministers is welcome. The
Dutch have often been particularly keen to work closely with the UK, only
to be deterred in the Conservative years by British standoffishness. The
British and the Dutch have similar views on the virtues of free trade,
liberal labour markets and EU budgetary discipline, as well as the
importance of healthy transatlantic relations. The fact that Mr Blair gets
on well with Wim Kok, the Dutch prime minister, offers scope for closer
links between Britain and Holland.

Denmark, Finland and Sweden are particularly suitable allies for a Labour
government. Their emphasis on a strong EU environmental policy and on
more transparent EU institutions resonates with at least some figures in
the Labour government. The Nordic trio are suspicious of Franco-German
efforts to deepen the EU's political union and have to contend with
relatively sceptical public opinions. They support the EU's economic
reform agenda, particularly measures to improve the supply-side. And
they are usually governed by social democratic parties of the sort that are
culturally quite close to Labour.

Britain should not ignore East European governments, some of which will
be potential allies once they are in the EU. Many of these governments
believe that France and Germany are much more interested than Britain
in developing economic, political and cultural ties with Eastern Europe.
Britain's embassy in Prague has a staff of 20, less than half the number
at the French and German embassies. Officials in the Polish Ministry of
Defence complain that, while they would like to establish links with their
opposite numbers in Britain, only the French and the Germans are willing
to co-operate. The Polish prime minister, Jerzy Buzek, elected in
September 1997, has visited all the major EU capitals except London. At
the time of writing he had not received an invitation.

One way for the Labour government to strengthen ties with the continent
is to work with fellow socialists. Mr Blair began by being rather suspicious
of contacts with other European socialists and has spent less time at Party
of European Socialists (PES) gatherings than some of the other socialist
prime ministers. Robin Cook appeared much keener on these events.

While there are obvious ideological differences between the EU's various
socialist governments, the Labour government could use the PES as a useful

network for reinforcing its influence. Socialist ministers have started to hold informal caucuses before meetings of the Council of Ministers. Come October, Britain, France, Italy, Holland, Finland, Denmark, Portugal, Greece and perhaps Germany and Sweden will have left-of-centre governments. Even a New Labour government shares some traditions, policies, priorities and values with these countries' socialist parties.

In the late 1980s and early 1990s informal caucuses of the European Peoples' Party (the christian democrats), under Mr Kohl's leadership, became an important influence on EU summits. The infamous decision of the November 1990 Rome summit to set a date for EMU—which began the chain of events leading to Mrs Thatcher's downfall—was hatched, in part, among informal gatherings of christian democrats. Usually, however, the most valuable aspect of such gatherings is simply that leaders get to know each other. It therefore becomes easier for them to present ideas and policies in ways that are likely to attract support.

As one of the stronger and more charismatic left-of-centre leaders, Mr Blair has a tremendous opportunity—if he is prepared to make some effort—to become the dominant socialist in the way that Mr Kohl led the christian democrats. In his second year of office Mr Blair seemed to view contacts with fellow socialists rather more warmly than he had done. His close aide Peter Mandelson, both before and after he became secretary of state for trade and industry, helped to nurture ties with continental socialists. Mr Mandelson was frequently spotted at seminars bringing together left-of-centre politicians and thinkers in France, Germany and Italy.

But while informal gatherings of like-minded leaders could prove useful, medium-term alliances with other member-states offer more potential. Britain will not be able to form such alliances unless it changes its methods and style of doing business in the EU. It has to win a reputation for trustworthiness. And British ministers have to understood that they will not win friends unless they sometimes give ground on an issue that matters to a prospective ally but is not that important to Britain. It is true that such package deals are more easily struck among countries that accept the same fundamental goals, while the British do not necessarily share the view of the six original members, plus Spain, Ireland, Greece and Portugal, that European integration is essentially a good thing.

Be that as it may, the fact is that many EU countries would like to team up with the British. So long as British ministers are willing to make an effort to understand the thinking of other governments, they will be able to forge alliances. For example, Britain might agree to back the Nordic countries in their campaign for greater openness, in return for their acquiescing to British proposals for reforming the EU's foreign policy machinery. Such alliance-building would certainly be easier if the British government—as suggested earlier in this booklet—could work out a clearer idea of what kind of EU it wants.

The construction of alliances would require Britain, on occasion, to give up some of its negotiating positions. The tabloids would be livid. But it should not be beyond the wit of Labour's spin doctors to explain to the tabloids that the point of such tactics is, in the long run, to increase British influence. A forward-looking strategy, combined with some crafty alliance-making, could make Britain not the dominant EU member, but one which counts. And that is a message that should be sellable to tabloids.

Ministers must understand that they need to please two audiences. Of course they have to worry about domestic constituencies, including tabloid editors, if they are to be re-elected. But in order to promote British interests in the EU they also have to think about how other governments will react to what they do and say.

If making friends is one thing Mr Blair has to do in order to make Britain a country that counts, the second is to take a more positive stance on the euro. His attitude to EMU, more than anything, will determine the degree to which Paris, Bonn and other capitals take Britain seriously. Britain has to appear to be on the road—however slow and circuitous that particular route may be—to monetary union. If Britain's partners thought it unlikely to join, the best bridging strategy imaginable could not prevent Britain's relegation to the outer rim of a two-speed Europe. The gap would be too wide to bridge. Neither a comprehensive effort to win allies, nor a plethora of proposals for plugging the democratic deficit, nor a clear vision of the kind of Europe it wants would suffice to restore Britain's position. Britain's influence over a whole range of areas—such as reform of the budget, farm policy and regional policy—would diminish, however sensible the policies it proposed. Britain can be a leading member of the European Union, so long as Tony Blair makes it clear that his government intends to join the euro.

A new British identity

In the long run, a stronger British role in Europe will depend not only on the government changing the way it deals with the EU, for example through forging alliances with other members. It will also depend on the British people learning to view the EU in a different way. They tend to see the EU as the kind of zero sum game that John Major had in mind when he proclaimed "game, set and match to Britain" on returning from the Maastricht summit. So long as the British people think that their gain is someone else's loss, and vice versa, their governments will be constrained in pursuing more positive European policies.

In most other EU countries people regard the Union as a positive sum game in which what is good for one country is often good for all of them. An underlying reason for this contrast is that, as Anthony Barnett has argued, Britons tend to see national identity in a different way from other Europeans. In much of the continent, national identity contains a strong European element. The French use the EU to give them a sense of grandeur on the world stage that they can no longer obtain on their own. The Germans love the EU for containing the nationalism that bedevilled their past. The Italians admire the EU for imposing efficient financial management on their government. The Spaniards still view the EU as a symbol of modernity and freedom from a Francoist past. The Irish nation could not become truly independent until the EU gave it the political recognition and the resources which allowed it to flourish. And so on.

But fewer Britons feel that the EU is anything to do with British identity. This is for reasons of geography and, above all, history: in this century Britain's history has had relatively few utterly shameful episodes. Not many Britons believe that their country needs the EU in order to be whole or respectable.

Thus a crucial but extremely difficult task for Tony Blair's government is to nudge the way the British perceive themselves in a European direction. Ministers have a responsibility to explain that what is good for other EU countries will often be good for Britain, and vice versa. But even the cleverest of spin doctors will find this an uphill struggle so long as many Britons think the EU is a distant, undemocratic and ineffective organisation.

Hence the importance of reforming the EU so that it becomes more open and accountable (as discussed in Chapter 5). If the British can start to imagine that the EU belongs to them, they will find it easier to realise that, over a host of areas—such as the fight against crime, the strength of the economy, social protection, environmental quality and influence in the world—Britain can only gain from working with its partners and those unloved but necessary EU institutions.

7 A summary of recommendations

The preceding sections contain a number of recommendations to the British government, to other EU governments and to the European institutions. Some of them are, in summary:

In the short term:
★ The British government should clarify its intentions over monetary union, stating that, so long as various economic criteria are met, it will seek to join shortly after the next general election (see page 23).

★ To prepare for joining the euro, the government should change its instructions to the Bank of England, so that it follows an exchange rate rather than an inflation target. The government should consider ways of encouraging borrowers to switch from floating-rate to fixed-rate mortgages (see page 25).

★ The European Central Bank must make every effort to explain its monetary policy to the people of Europe. Its board members should report, in person and frequently, to a committee of European and national parliamentarians. The ECB should also publish minutes of board meetings soon after the event (see page 59).

★ To help make the governance of Europe more transparent, the Council of Ministers should be televised when it meets as a legislature. EU institutions should post as many documents as possible on the internet, and welcome public responses (see page 58).

★ The European Parliament's budgetary control committee should play a greater role in monitoring EU spending and in rooting out fraud. It needs more resources and the right to summon national officials. It should consider establishing specialist sub-committees for each principal area of spending. The budgetary control committee should work more closely with the EU's Court of Auditors (see page 64).

★ Britain should push the Commission to develop a European
consumers' agenda. For example, EU rules on selective distribution
practices should be reformed, so that manufacturers cannot maintain
the prices of some trademarked goods by preventing their sale in
supermarkets (see page 29).

★ In order to improve the independence of EU competition policy,
the Commission's competition directorate should publish every
report before it is discussed by commissioners. If the commissioners
then wished to over-rule the directorate's recommendations, they
would have to issue a public explanation (see page 29).

★ In areas of policy where binding, centrally-set rules are not essential,
the Union should be readier to rely on peer-group pressure. The
Council of Ministers should set objectives, leaving each government to
fulfil them as best it can, in the light of best practice. The Commission
and Parliament could then monitor progress (see page 57).

★ Britain should be more positive on justice and home affairs co-
operation. It should opt in to the EU's common asylum policies,
work to strengthen Europol and encourage the mutual recognition
of court decisions (see page 38).

★ In order to give the Union a more coherent and effective voice in
foreign policy, EU governments should appoint a heavyweight
politician, rather than a diplomat, as their "high representative"
for foreign policy. The foreign ministries' "political directors" should
be based in Brussels rather than in national capitals. Britain and
France should make it clear that, if the United States pulls its troops
out of Bosnia, they are prepared to lead a European peacekeeping
force there (see pages 43 & 46).

★ To ensure that the Union's enlargement into Eastern Europe does not
grind to a halt, it should set a deadline of 2004 for the entry of the
first new members—so long as they can meet the required criteria.
And governments should conclude an agreement on the reform of
the Union's budget, farm policy and structural funds by the end of
the German presidency in June 1999 (see page 35).

And in the longer term:

★ Britain should maximise its influence by pursuing alliances with other member-states. This will require a greater willingness than in the past to cede ground on some points, in order to gain the support of other members on the issues which matter most to Britain. As a start Britain should seek to improve relations with France and Germany by shadowing many of the provisions of the Elysée treaty with each of them (see page 78).

★ Britain should oppose the development of a "two-speed" Europe, whereby participation in EMU determines whether a country is a first-class or a second-class EU member. As the Union expands into Eastern Europe, Britain should favour the development of flexible constitutional structures which allow countries to join some aspects of the Union but not others (see page 17).

★ The abolition of the Western European Union would strengthen both NATO and the European Union. The WEU's military tasks should be transferred to NATO and its political role to a fourth pillar of the European Union. The Union's defence ministers would be able to instruct European forces within NATO to embark on EU military missions (see page 47).

★ In order to reduce some of the gap that separates ordinary people from EU institutions, the voters of each country should elect their own European commissioner. The European Council would choose one of the commissioners as president. The European Parliament would be able to sack individual commissioners, on a two thirds vote. To ensure that commissioners did not pander to national interests, their terms of office would be non-renewable (see page 67).